Better Homes and Gardens®

MAKE NOW SERVE LATER
recipes

© 1981 by Meredith Corporation, Des Moines, Iowa.
All Rights Reserved. Printed in the United States of America.
Large-Format Edition. Second Printing, 1983.
Library of Congress Catalog Card Number: 80-68453
ISBN: 0-696-01350-9

Credits

On the cover:
Stuffed Chicken Rolls (see recipe, page 35)
Cheese Manicotti (see recipe, page 44)
Beef Turnovers (see recipe, page 9)

Better Homes and Gardens® Books
Editor: Gerald M. Knox
Art Director: Ernest Shelton

Food and Nutrition Editor: Doris Eby
Senior Food Editor: Sharyl Heiken
Senior Associate Food Editors: Sandra Granseth, Elizabeth Woolever
Associate Food Editors: Bonnie Lasater, Julia Martinusen, Diana McMillen,
  Marcia Stanley, Diane Yanney
Recipe Development Editor: Marion Viall
Test Kitchen Director: Sharon Stilwell
Test Kitchen Home Economists: Jean Brekke, Kay Cargill, Marilyn Cornelius,
  Maryellyn Krantz, Marge Steenson

Associate Art Directors: Neoma Alt West, Randall Yontz
Copy and Production Editors: David Kirchner, Lamont Olson, David A. Walsh
Assistant Art Director: Harijs Priekulis
Senior Graphic Designer: Faith Berven
Graphic Designers: Alisann Dixon, Linda Ford, Lynda Haupert,
  Lyne Neymeyer, Tom Wegner

Editor in Chief: Neil Kuehnl
Group Administrative Editor: Duane Gregg
Executive Art Director: William J. Yates

General Manager: Fred Stines
Director of Publishing: Robert B. Nelson
Director of Retail Marketing: Jamie Martin
Director of Direct Marketing: Arthur Heydendael

Make Now, Serve Later Recipes
Editor: Diana McMillen
Copy and Production Editor: Lamont Olson
Graphic Designer: Lynda Haupert

Our seal assures you that every recipe in
Make Now, Serve Later Recipes is endorsed
by the Better Homes and Gardens
Test Kitchen. Each recipe is tested for
family appeal, practicality, and deliciousness.

Contents

Introduction

Cooking When You Can

You can serve delicious, home-cooked meals even when your schedule is busy. The recipes in this book give you the freedom to cook foods one day and serve them another.

Recipes are designed to be prepared ahead and stored in the refrigerator, in the freezer, or on your kitchen shelf until a later meal or snack. To make good use of your time, prepare a main dish one night, refrigerate it, and serve it the next day. Or, cook a quantity of food on a weekend to freeze and serve in the weeks to come.

Select a recipe with a storage method that fits your schedule. Refrigerated recipes can be stored for as long as 24 hours. For longer storage, try a freezer recipe and see the Freezer Guide on pages 58 and 59 to determine the maximum storage time.

Each recipe indicates the advance preparation and the final preparation before serving. Although the time required for advance preparation varies, the work involved for last-minute preparation has been reduced to a minimum, all designed to be easy on the cook.

Make Now, Serve Later Recipes also includes make-ahead hints, special double-duty recipes, a menu chapter, and chapters of main dish, side dish, dessert, and snack and beverage recipes. All were created to give you a break from the kitchen when you need it most.

Make-Ahead Hints

You can reduce hectic last-min-ute food preparation by follow-ing the make-ahead tips on this page. When you plan and pre-pare ahead, you'll find that meals can be enjoyable even on the busiest days.

● Plan meals for several days or a week in advance. Planned meals help you make only one shopping trip to ensure you have all the nec-essary ingredients. This helps eliminate wasted time spent on un-necessary trips.

● Before preparing a make-ahead food, read the recipe carefully to determine what ingredients are needed at serving time. If it's a refrigerator recipe, buy all the in-gredients at once. If it's a freezer recipe, buy just the ingredients needed for advance preparation.

● When entertaining, choose a menu that includes some foods that can be prepared well in ad-vance. Last-minute foods should be easy to fix so you can spend as much time with your guests as possible.

● Serve a make-ahead, one-dish meal such as meat and vegetable combinations. While it's baking, prepare a simple salad or a quick dessert as an accompaniment.

● When cooking frozen meat mix-tures, you can speed thawing by stirring frequently. Stir gently to avoid breaking up food.

● For easy separation, stack ground meat patties with 2 layers of waxed paper between. Cover with moisture-vaporproof wrap; seal, label, and freeze. Before serving, simply remove the desired number of patties from the freezer without having to pry them apart.

● Shortcut the last-minute prepa-ration of stuffed meats or poultry by preparing the stuffing mixture ahead. Cover and refrigerate the stuffing separately from the meat. At serving time, stuff the meat and then bake.

● Make use of leftovers by placing servings in the compartments of divided foil trays. The individual frozen dinners can be reheated in the oven for a no-fuss meal. Check the Freezer Guide on pages 58 and 59 when selecting cooked foods to freeze.

● Hard-cook eggs several at a time so they'll be ready to use in salads and casseroles, or for a quick, nutritious snack. Store hard-cooked eggs in the refrigerator for as long as one week.

● Prepare bread crumbs in a large quantity by blending leftover bread slices in a blender container or food processor bowl. Store the bread crumbs in the refrigerator or freezer to use as a quick last-min-ute casserole topper.

● Choose cookware that you can use for more than one job, such as freezer-to-oven-to-table baking dishes and casseroles, and oven-going skillets.

● Serve more cold meals that can be prepared ahead. This includes make-ahead salads, sandwiches, and soups. They're just as appe-tizing, and they don't require reheating.

● Vegetables used in make-ahead casseroles are best if slightly un-dercooked during the advance preparation. The vegetables finish cooking when the casserole is baked before serving.

● To speed last-minute tossed salad preparation, clean salad in-gredients and chop firm vegeta-bles such as carrots, celery, and green peppers early in the day. Wrap and chill vegetables till serv-ing time.

● Unless salad ingredients need to marinate in the dressing mixture, cover and chill salad dressing sep-arately. Lightly toss dressing with salad just before serving.

● Fruit and nut breads generally improve in flavor when baked a day or two before serving. To pre-pare nut bread sandwiches ahead, thinly slice bread and spread with softened cream cheese, butter, or margarine. Freeze the sandwiches until they are needed.

5

Make-Ahead Menus

This time-saving menu section will give you spare time when it's most needed — just before serving a meal. Choose from recipe combinations that are as formal as the dinner party on pages 8 and 9 or as casual as the picnic menu on page 12.

Menu recipes are coordinated to make the best use of your time. Some recipes can be prepared a week in advance, while others are made the night before.

The menus also include suggestions for purchased foods to round out the meal, hints for scheduling recipe preparation, and some recipe options.

Plan ahead so entertaining and family meals can be easy by using the suggestions in this chapter of Make-Ahead Menus.

Herbed Julienne Vegetables
Almond and Fruit Salad
Beef Turnovers
Mocha Caramel Custard
(see recipes, pages 8 and 9)

Dinner Party

Host a make-ahead dinner party and you'll wonder why you didn't do it this way before. With this dinner menu you can prepare the Beef Turnovers as much as a week in advance. The day before the party you can make the vegetables, salad, and dessert. With only minor last-minute preparation, you're free to spend time with your guests.

MENU

Beef Turnovers

Herbed Julienne Vegetables

Almond & Fruit Salad

Mocha Caramel Custard or Praline Mousse

Beverage

Praline Mousse

- ¼ cup packed brown sugar
- 1 envelope unflavored gelatin
- ⅛ teaspoon salt
- ¾ cup cold water
- 3 beaten egg yolks
- ⅓ cup praline liqueur *or* Amaretto
- 3 egg whites
- ¼ cup sugar
- 1 cup whipping cream
- 3 tablespoons chopped pecans

For collar, fold a 23x9-inch piece of waxed paper lengthwise into thirds. Butter one side of the paper. Attach paper, buttered side in, around the top of a 1-quart soufflé dish so that the paper extends 2 inches above the dish. Fasten with tape. (Or, use individual soufflé dishes without collars.)

In saucepan combine brown sugar, gelatin, and salt. Stir in cold water. Stir over low heat till sugar and gelatin are dissolved. Stir *half* of hot mixture into beaten egg yolks; return all to saucepan. Cook and stir over low heat 2 to 3 minutes or till slightly thickened. *Do not boil.* Remove from heat; stir in liqueur. Chill till the consistency of corn syrup, stirring occasionally. Immediately beat egg whites till soft peaks form (tips curl over); gradually add the sugar, beating till stiff peaks form (tips stand straight). Whip cream till soft peaks form. When the gelatin mixture is partially set (the consistency of unbeaten egg whites), fold beaten egg whites and whipped cream into gelatin mixture. Turn into prepared soufflé dish or individual dishes. Refrigerate at least 6 hours or till firm.

Before serving: Remove collar; sprinkle top and sides with pecans. Makes 6 to 8 servings.

Herbed Julienne Vegetables

Pictured on pages 6 and 7 —

- 3 medium carrots, cut into julienne strips (about 1 cup)
- 6 stalks celery, cut into julienne strips (about 3 cups)
- 2 tablespoons butter *or* margarine, melted
- 2 teaspoons lemon juice
- ½ teaspoon dried basil, crushed
- ¼ teaspoon salt

In covered saucepan cook carrots and celery in boiling salted water about 10 minutes or just till tender. Drain. Combine the melted butter or margarine, lemon juice, basil, and salt; drizzle over carrots and celery. Cover and refrigerate for 2 to 24 hours.

Before serving: Cook, covered, over low heat till heated through. Makes 6 servings.

Dinner Party

Beef Turnovers

Pictured on pages 6 and 7 —

3 cups all-purpose flour
1 teaspoon salt
¾ cup shortening
1⅓ cups cream-style cottage cheese, sieved
1½ pounds beef round steak, cut into ¼-inch cubes (3½ cups)
½ of a 10-ounce package frozen chopped spinach, cooked and well drained
¾ cup shredded Swiss cheese (3 ounces)
1 medium potato, peeled and cut into ¼-inch cubes (¾ cup)
1 medium carrot, finely chopped
½ cup finely chopped onion
1½ teaspoons instant beef bouillon granules
¼ teaspoon dried thyme, crushed
¼ teaspoon dried marjoram, crushed
¼ teaspoon pepper
1 beaten egg
⅓ cup catsup *or* hot-style catsup
2 tablespoons water
1 tablespoon steak sauce

To make pastry, in mixing bowl stir together flour and salt. Cut in shortening till mixture resembles small peas. Add cottage cheese. Toss with fork till moistened. Form into a ball.

For meat filling, combine beef, spinach, Swiss cheese, potato, carrot, onion, bouillon granules, thyme, marjoram, and pepper; mix well. Divide pastry dough into 6 equal portions. On lightly floured surface roll each portion into an 8-inch square. Spoon about ¾ cup of the meat filling into the center of *each* square.

Moisten edges of each pastry square. Fold all 4 corners of each square to the center. Seal edges. Place in a greased 15x10x1-inch baking pan. Cover with moisture-vaporproof wrap. Seal, label, and freeze.

Before serving: Brush with beaten egg. Bake in 375° oven about 1¼ hours or till done. Meanwhile, combine catsup, water, and steak sauce; heat through. Pass sauce with turnovers. Serves 6.

Almond and Fruit Salad

Pictured on pages 6 and 7 —

1 15½-ounce can pineapple chunks
3 medium oranges, peeled, sectioned, and drained
1 kiwi, peeled and sliced
¼ cup honey
1 teaspoon finely shredded orange peel
Fresh spinach
Sliced almonds

Drain pineapple chunks, reserving 2 tablespoons syrup. In bowl combine pineapple chunks, orange sections, and kiwi slices. Stir together reserved pineapple syrup, honey, and orange peel; pour over fruit in bowl. Toss lightly. Cover and refrigerate for 2 to 24 hours.

Before serving: Spoon into individual spinach-lined bowls. Garnish with sliced almonds. Makes 6 servings.

Mocha Caramel Custard

Pictured on pages 6 and 7 —

½ cup sugar
2½ cups milk
½ cup sugar
1 square (1 ounce) semisweet chocolate
½ teaspoon instant coffee crystals
Dash salt
3 beaten eggs
3 tablespoons coffee liqueur
Chocolate curls (optional)

In a heavy 10-inch skillet stir ½ cup sugar over medium heat for 8 to 10 minutes or till melted and golden brown; remove from heat. Immediately divide melted sugar between six 6-ounce custard cups, swirling to coat bottoms. Set aside. In same skillet combine milk, ½ cup sugar, chocolate, coffee crystals, and salt. Stir over medium heat till sugar is dissolved and chocolate is melted. (If mixture is flecked with chocolate, beat with a rotary beater 1 minute to mix well.) Remove from heat; cool about 15 minutes.

Combine cooled milk mixture, eggs, and coffee liqueur. Pour into custard cups; place cups in a 13x9x2-inch baking pan. Pour hot water into pan around custard cups to a depth of 1 inch. Bake in 325° oven for 30 to 35 minutes or till knife inserted just off-center comes out clean. Cool. Cover and refrigerate for 2 to 24 hours.

Before serving: If desired, loosen custard around edges; invert onto plate. If desired, garnish with chocolate curls. Makes 6 servings.

Cocktail Party

With the help of these make-ahead cocktail party recipes, you'll have time to mingle with your guests instead of preparing food in the kitchen. Some of the dishes can be prepared in advance and chilled, while others are made ahead, stored, and then heated at the last minute. Arrange your serving table before guests arrive and you'll have nothing left to do but savor the evening.

MENU

Chicken & Ham Pinwheels

Barbecue-Sauced Meatballs

Smoky Cheese Ball or Cheesy Wheat Germ Spread

Dijon Vegetable Antipasto

Curried Peanuts with Raisins

Bubbly Rosé Punch or Coffee

Smoky Cheese Ball

1 cup shredded smoked cheddar cheese (4 ounces)
1 cup shredded American cheese (4 ounces)
1 3-ounce package cream cheese with chives, softened
3 tablespoons mayonnaise
2 teaspoons lemon juice
1 teaspoon Worcestershire sauce
Dash bottled hot pepper sauce
Chopped walnuts
Snipped parsley
Assorted crackers

Bring cheddar and American cheeses to room temperature. In mixer bowl beat together cream cheese, mayonnaise, lemon juice, Worcestershire sauce, and hot pepper sauce on medium speed of electric mixer. Beat in cheddar and American cheeses. Chill at least 1 hour. Shape cheese mixture into a ball; garnish with chopped walnuts and snipped parsley, pressing lightly over outside of ball. Wrap in clear plastic wrap. Refrigerate for 3 to 24 hours. (Or, seal, label, and freeze.)

Before serving: If frozen, thaw 2 hours at room temperature. Unwrap; serve with assorted crackers. Makes 1 ball.

Barbecue-Sauced Meatballs

1 beaten egg
2 tablespoons milk
¾ cup soft bread crumbs (1 slice)
2 tablespoons finely chopped onion
½ teaspoon salt
½ teaspoon ground sage
⅛ teaspoon garlic powder
1 pound lean ground beef
¾ cup bottled barbecue sauce
⅓ cup orange marmalade
⅓ cup water

For meatballs, in bowl combine egg and milk. Stir in bread crumbs, onion, salt, sage, and garlic powder. Add meat; mix well. Shape into 1-inch meatballs; place in a shallow baking pan. Bake in a 350° oven for 15 to 18 minutes or till done. Drain on paper toweling.

Meanwhile, combine barbecue sauce, orange marmalade, and water. Stir in meatballs. Turn into a 1-quart freezer container. Cover, seal, label, and freeze.

Before serving: In saucepan cook meatball mixture over medium-low heat about 40 minutes or till heated through, stirring occasionally with fork to separate. Skim off excess fat. Serve meatballs hot with wooden picks. Makes 42.

● **Microwave directions:** Prepare and freeze Barbecue-Sauced Meatballs as directed above. Place frozen mixture in a 2-quart nonmetal casserole. Cook, covered, in a counter-top microwave oven on high power 10 to 12 minutes or till heated through, stirring 2 or 3 times with a fork to separate. Serve as directed above.

Cocktail Party

Bubbly Rosé Punch

3 cups cranberry juice cocktail
1 6-ounce can frozen
    lemonade concentrate
8 inches stick cinnamon,
    broken
4 whole cloves
1 750-milliliter bottle rosé wine
2 12-ounce cans lemon-lime
    carbonated beverage,
    chilled
    Ice cubes

Heat cranberry juice, lemonade concentrate, cinnamon, and cloves. Bring to boiling; simmer, uncovered, 10 minutes. Strain spices. Stir in wine. Cover and refrigerate 3 to 24 hours.

Before serving: Pour wine mixture into a pitcher or a punch bowl. Stir in carbonated beverage; add ice cubes. Garnish with orange slices, if desired. Makes 19 (4-ounce) servings.

Curried Peanuts with Raisins

2 tablespoons cooking oil
1 to 2 teaspoons curry powder
1 12-ounce package (2 cups)
    raw peanuts
¾ cup raisins

Combine oil, curry powder, and ½ teaspoon *salt.* Stir in peanuts; mix well. Spread into a 13x9x2-inch baking pan. Bake in 350° oven about 25 minutes or till nuts are lightly browned. Cool. Stir in raisins. Store, covered, at room temperature. Makes 2¾ cups.

Cheesy Wheat Germ Spread

1 cup shredded cheddar
    cheese
⅓ cup mayonnaise
1 teaspoon lemon juice
1 teaspoon Worcestershire
    sauce
½ cup finely chopped apple
½ cup finely shredded carrot
¼ cup finely chopped celery
¼ cup chopped walnuts
2 tablespoons chopped raisins
1 tablespoon finely chopped
    green pepper
1 tablespoon wheat germ
    Whole wheat *or* rye bread,
    diagonally cut into quarters
    and crusts removed

Bring cheese to room temperature. Combine cheese, and next 3 ingredients. Beat till smooth. Fold in apple, carrot, celery, walnuts, raisins, green pepper, and wheat germ. Cover; refrigerate 3 to 24 hours.

Before serving: Stir to blend ingredients. Serve on bread triangles. Makes 2 cups spread.

Dijon Vegetable Antipasto

⅓ cup olive *or* salad oil
3 tablespoons lemon juice
2 tablespoons Dijon-style
    mustard
3½ to 4 cups fresh vegetables★
    Sliced prosciutto, rolled up

In jar combine oil, lemon juice, mustard, ½ teaspoon *salt,* and ¼ teaspoon *pepper.* Cover; shake. Add vegetables. Cover tightly and invert. Refrigerate for 3 to 24 hours, inverting jar occasionally.

Before serving: Drain vegetables. Arrange on platter with prosciutto. Makes 10 to 12 appetizer servings.

★ **Vegetable options:** Use any of the following: halved mushrooms; cauliflower flowerets; Chinese pea pods; sliced cucumbers, zucchini, or yellow summer squash; *or* halved cherry tomatoes.

Chicken and Ham Pinwheels

2 whole chicken breasts,
    skinned and boned
¼ teaspoon dried basil, crushed
    Dash garlic powder
3 slices boiled ham (3 ounces)
2 teaspoons lemon juice
    Paprika
    Party whole wheat bread
    Butter *or* margarine
    Prepared mustard

Place chicken, boned side up, between 2 pieces of clear plastic wrap. Pound to ¼-inch thickness. Remove wrap. Combine basil, garlic powder, ¼ teaspoon *salt,* and dash *pepper;* sprinkle on chicken. Cover each with 1½ *slices* ham; roll up lengthwise.

Place, seam down, in 10x6x2-inch baking dish. Drizzle with lemon juice; sprinkle with paprika. Bake in 350° oven 35 to 40 minutes. Cover; refrigerate 3 to 24 hours.

Before serving: Cut rolls into ¼-inch thick slices. Serve on bread slices spread with butter and mustard. Makes 24 slices.

Picnic

Serve this delightful picnic spread without much preparation on picnic day. Make the custard sauce several days in advance and it will keep in your freezer. The day before the picnic, prepare the chicken, coleslaw, relishes, and the beverage. Then pack your plates, silverware, napkins, and bread. When picnic day arrives, all you have to do is prepare the fruit, pack the cooler, and you're ready to go.

MENU

Sesame Fried Chicken

Garden Coleslaw

Assorted Relishes

Bread w/ Butter

Fruit w/ Custard Sauce

Beverage

Garden Coleslaw

　3　cups shredded cabbage
　½　cup chopped green pepper
　⅓　cup finely shredded carrot
　2　green onions, sliced
　¼　cup vinegar
　2 to 3　tablespoons sugar
　2　tablespoons salad oil
　½　teaspoon dry mustard

Combine shredded cabbage, green pepper, carrot, and onions. In screw-top jar combine vinegar, sugar, salad oil, mustard, and ½ teaspoon *salt;* shake well. Pour over vegetables; toss. Cover and refrigerate for 3 to 24 hours.

Before serving: Store, covered, in cooler. Toss before serving. Makes 6 servings.

Sesame Fried Chicken

　¼　cup finely crushed rich round crackers
　¼　cup grated Parmesan cheese
　¼　cup sesame seed, toasted
　2　teaspoons dried parsley flakes
　¼　teaspoon paprika
　1　slightly beaten egg
　1　2½- to 3-pound broiler-fryer chicken, cut up

Combine cracker crumbs, Parmesan cheese, sesame seed, parsley, paprika, and ¼ teaspoon *salt.* Combine egg and 1 tablespoon water. Dip chicken in egg mixture; roll in cracker mixture.

Arrange chicken, skin side up, in baking pan so pieces don't touch. Bake, uncovered, in a 375° oven for 1 hour. Cool slightly. Remove from pan. Cover and refrigerate for 3 to 24 hours.

Before serving: To transport, store covered chicken in cooler. Makes 6 servings.

Fruit with Custard Sauce

　3　beaten egg yolks
　⅓　cup Marsala wine
　¼　cup sugar
　½　cup whipping cream
　3　cups berries, cubed melon, *and/or* sliced peaches *or* plums

In top of double boiler combine yolks and wine. Stir in sugar and dash *salt.* Place over boiling water (water in bottom of double boiler should not touch top pan). Beat constantly for 6 to 8 minutes or till thickened. Place pan in larger pan of ice water. Beat 2 to 3 minutes. Whip cream to soft peaks; fold into yolk mixture. Turn into freezer container. Cover, seal, label, and freeze.

Before serving: Remove sauce from freezer. Thaw in refrigerator or picnic cooler about 3 hours. Stir gently; spoon sauce over fruit. Makes 6 servings.

Sesame Fried Chicken
Garden Coleslaw
Quick bread
Fruit with Custard Sauce
Assorted relishes

Buffet

Let your guests serve themselves with this buffet-style dinner. Plan ahead and prepare the food as your schedule permits. You can do all the make-ahead preparation the day before, or stretch it out over a couple of days. Either way, with a few last-minute touches, everyone can enjoy a no-hurry dinner.

MENU

Tomato Refresher

Lasagna Rolls

Spinach & Mushroom Salad

Date-Nut Bread with Cinnamon Honey Butter

Crepes Nesselrode

Beverage

Crepes Nesselrode

¼ cup raisins
2 tablespoons rum
⅓ cup sugar
1 tablespoon all-purpose flour
1 tablespoon cornstarch
¼ teaspoon salt
1½ cups milk
1 slightly beaten egg yolk
1 teaspoon vanilla
½ cup whipping cream
½ cup diced mixed candied fruits and peels
½ cup chopped pecans, toasted
12 Dessert Crepes
Candied cherries

Soak raisins in rum for 1 hour; set aside. To make custard, in small saucepan combine sugar, flour, cornstarch, and salt. Gradually stir in milk. Cook and stir till mixture is thickened and bubbly. Cook and stir 1 to 2 minutes more. Stir *half* the hot mixture into egg yolk; return all to hot mixture. Bring mixture to gentle boil. Cook and stir 2 minutes more. Remove from heat. Stir in vanilla. Cover surface with waxed paper or clear plastic wrap. Cool without stirring. Whip cream to soft peaks; fold into cooled custard. Drain raisins. Stir raisins, candied fruits and peels, and the pecans into custard.

To assemble, spoon about ¼ *cup* custard filling on the un-browned side of each Dessert Crepe. Roll crepe around filling to make a cornucopia shape. Place crepes in a 13x9x2-inch baking dish. Cover and refrigerate 2 to 24 hours.

Before serving: Garnish each filled crepe with candied cherries. Makes 12 servings.

Dessert Crepes: In a bowl combine 1½ cups *milk,* 1 cup all-purpose *flour,* 2 *eggs,* 2 tablespoons *sugar,* 1 tablespoon *cooking oil,* and ⅛ teaspoon *salt;* beat with a rotary beater till well combined. Heat a lightly greased 6-inch skillet. Remove from heat. Spoon in 2 *tablespoons* batter; lift and tilt skillet to spread batter. Return to heat; brown on one side. Invert pan over paper toweling; remove crepe. Repeat to make 16 to 18 crepes, greasing skillet as necessary. Freeze any extra crepes by stacking crepes and alternating double layers of waxed paper. Overwrap with moisture-vaporproof wrap. Seal, label, and freeze.

Cinnamon Honey Butter

½ cup butter *or* margarine, softened
2 teaspoons honey
¼ teaspoon ground cinnamon

In small mixer bowl beat butter or margarine on low speed of electric mixer till fluffy. Add honey and cinnamon; beat till light. Turn mixture into a small crock or bowl. Cover and refrigerate 2 to 24 hours.

Before serving: Let butter mixture stand at room temperature for 15 minutes. Serve with bread. Makes about ½ cup.

Buffet

Lasagna Rolls

16 lasagna noodles
1½ pounds ground pork *used itl sausag*
 1 medium onion, chopped (½ cup)
 1 beaten egg
 1 cup cream-style cottage cheese
½ cup grated Parmesan cheese
¼ cup snipped parsley
 1 teaspoon dried basil, crushed
 1 cup shredded mozzarella cheese (4 ounces)
 2 8-ounce cans pizza sauce
¼ cup dry red wine

In a large kettle or Dutch oven cook lasagna noodles in a large amount of boiling salted water for 10 to 12 minutes or just till tender. Drain well. Rinse noodles with cold water; drain.

In skillet cook ground pork and chopped onion till meat is browned and onion is tender. Drain off fat. In bowl combine egg, cottage cheese, Parmesan cheese, parsley, and basil; stir into meat mixture. Spread each strip of cooked pasta with about ¼ cup of the meat-cheese mixture. Roll up each strip jelly-roll style. Place pasta rolls, seam side down, in a greased 13x9x2-inch baking dish. Sprinkle mozzarella cheese over pasta rolls. Combine the pizza sauce and red wine; pour over cheese. Cover with moisture-vaporproof wrap. Seal, label, and freeze.

Before serving: Bake, covered, in a 400° oven about 1¼ hours or till heated through. Makes 8 servings.

Tomato Refresher

 3 cups tomato juice
 1 stalk celery, cut up
 1 slice onion
½ medium green pepper, cut up
½ teaspoon salt
  Few dashes bottled hot pepper sauce
  Few dashes Worcestershire sauce
  Celery stalks

In blender container combine tomato juice, cut-up celery, onion, green pepper, salt, hot pepper sauce, and Worcestershire sauce. Cover and blend just till vegetables are finely chopped. Refrigerate, covered, in blender container 2 to 24 hours.

Before serving: Blend, covered, just till mixed; pour into 8 chilled juice glasses. Garnish with celery stalks. Makes 8 (4-ounce) servings.

Date-Nut Bread

1½ cups all-purpose flour
½ cup sugar
 1 teaspoon baking soda
½ teaspoon baking powder
½ teaspoon salt
½ cup quick-cooking rolled oats
½ cup chopped walnuts
 1 beaten egg
 1 cup dairy sour cream
½ cup snipped pitted dates
¼ cup molasses

In bowl combine flour, sugar, baking soda, baking powder, and salt. Stir in rolled oats and chopped walnuts. In another bowl combine egg, sour cream, dates, and molasses; beat well. Add egg-sour cream mixture to dry ingredients; stir just till moistened.

Turn batter into a greased 8x4x2-inch loaf pan. Bake in a 350° oven for 40 to 45 minutes or till wooden pick inserted near center comes out clean. Cool in pan 10 minutes. Remove from pan; cool thoroughly on wire rack. Wrap in foil; refrigerate 3 to 24 hours.

Before serving: Cut bread into slices. Makes 1 loaf.

Spinach and Mushroom Salad

 1 clove garlic
 6 cups torn spinach
 1 cup sliced fresh mushrooms
½ cup sliced radishes
⅓ cup chopped carrot
¼ cup salad oil
¼ cup white wine vinegar
 1 tablespoon sugar
½ teaspoon salt

Using the back of a spoon, mash garlic in salad bowl. Add spinach, mushrooms, radishes, and carrot; toss lightly. Cover and refrigerate 2 to 24 hours.

In screw-top jar combine salad oil, white wine vinegar, sugar, and salt. Cover and shake to mix well. Refrigerate 2 to 24 hours.

Before serving: Shake dressing; pour over salad. Toss lightly. Makes 8 servings.

Family Gathering

You don't have to spend the day of a family gathering cooking in order to serve a meal. With this menu you can make the bread a week ahead of time, the meat and fudge sauce several days early, and everything else the day before. Then just 1½ hours before mealtime start cooking the meat. Add the broccoli 45 minutes later and the bread for the last 12 minutes. It's easy and you'll even have meat left over for another meal.

MENU

Sauerbraten

Broccoli Bake

Fruited Nectar Salad

Rye Bread Loaves with Butter

Hot Fudge Sundaes

Beverage

Sauerbraten

Sauerbraten is a German word meaning sour roast —

    2 cups water
    ½ cup dry red wine
    ½ cup red wine vinegar
    1 medium onion, thinly sliced
    4 whole cloves
    4 whole peppercorns
    2 bay leaves
    1 3-pound beef round rump
      roast
    2 tablespoons cooking oil *or*
      shortening
    ⅓ cup finely crushed
      gingersnaps (5)

To make marinade, in saucepan combine water, red wine, wine vinegar, onion, cloves, peppercorns, and bay leaves. Bring mixture to boiling; simmer for 5 minutes. Cool to room temperature. Place roast in large bowl; pour marinade over roast. Turn roast to coat all sides. Cover and refrigerate for 2 to 3 days, turning the roast at least twice a day.

Before serving: Remove roast from marinade; pat dry with paper toweling. Strain marinade to remove cloves, peppercorns, and bay leaves. In Dutch oven brown the rump roast in hot cooking oil or shortening. Drain off the fat. Add the strained marinade and simmer, covered, for 1½ to 1¾ hours or till the meat is tender. Add more water, if necessary.

Remove roast to platter. Pour the remaining marinade into a large measuring cup; skim off any fat. Add enough *water* to the remaining marinade to make 2 cups liquid. Return marinade to Dutch oven; stir in crushed gingersnaps. Cook and stir for 5 to 10 minutes or till the crumbs dissolve and the marinade mixture thickens. Cut the roast into thin slices; serve with the thickened marinade mixture. Makes 12 servings.

Fruited Nectar Salad

    1 12-ounce can apricot nectar
    1 3-ounce package lemon-
      flavored gelatin
    ½ cup cold water
    1 tablespoon lemon juice
    1 11-ounce can mandarin
      orange sections, drained
    ½ cup seedless green grapes,
      halved
    ¼ cup chopped apple
      Lettuce leaves
      Mayonnaise *or* salad
      dressing

In saucepan heat apricot nectar to boiling. Add lemon-flavored gelatin; stir till gelatin is dissolved. Stir in water and lemon juice. Chill till partially set (the consistency of unbeaten egg whites). Fold in oranges, grapes, and apple. Pour into a 3½-cup mold. Refrigerate at least 6 hours or till firm.

Before serving: Unmold onto lettuce-lined plate. Serve with mayonnaise or salad dressing. Makes 8 servings.

Rye Bread Loaves

You can freeze these brown-and-serve loaves individually, then use them as needed —

 1 package active dry yeast
 ¼ cup warm water (110° to 115°)
 2 cups milk
 2 tablespoons brown sugar
 1 tablespoon butter *or* margarine
 2 teaspoons salt
 1¾ cups rye flour
 3½ to 4 cups all-purpose flour
 Melted butter *or* margarine

Soften yeast in warm water. In saucepan heat milk, brown sugar, butter or margarine, and salt just till warm (115° to 120°) and butter is almost melted, stirring constantly. Turn into large mixing bowl. Stir in rye flour; beat well. Add softened yeast; stir till smooth. Stir in as much of the all-purpose flour as you can mix in with a spoon. Turn out onto lightly floured surface. Knead in enough of the remaining flour to make a moderately stiff dough that is smooth and elastic (6 to 8 minutes total). Place in lightly greased bowl; turn once to grease surface. Cover; let rise in warm place till double (about 1¼ hours).

Punch dough down; divide into 8 portions. Cover; let rest 10 minutes. Shape each portion into a loaf; place in 8 greased 4½x2½x1½-inch individual loaf pans. Cover; let rise in warm place till double, about 20 to 25 minutes. Bake loaves in 325° oven for 20 to 25 minutes. *Do not brown.* Remove from pan. Cool on wire rack.

Wrap in moisture-vaporproof wrap. Seal, label, and freeze.

Before serving: Thaw at room temperature for 10 to 15 minutes. Unwrap; brush with melted butter or margarine. Place on baking sheet. Bake the bread in 375° oven for 12 to 15 minutes or till golden. Makes 8 loaves.

Broccoli Bake

For a different flavor, substitute another shredded process cheese for the American cheese —

 2 10-ounce packages frozen cut broccoli
 1 10¾-ounce can condensed cream of mushroom soup
 1 cup shredded American cheese (4 ounces)
 ¼ cup mayonnaise *or* salad dressing
 ¼ cup milk
 ⅓ cup crushed round cheese crackers

Cook broccoli according to package directions, *except* omit salt; drain thoroughly. In bowl stir together cream of mushroom soup, shredded American cheese, mayonnaise or salad dressing, and milk; fold in cooked and drained broccoli. Turn into a 1-quart casserole. Cover and refrigerate 3 to 24 hours.

Before serving; Top broccoli mixture with crushed cheese crackers. Bake in a 375° oven for 45 to 50 minutes or till heated through. Makes 8 servings.

Hot Fudge Sundaes

 ¾ cup sugar
 3 tablespoons unsweetened cocoa powder
 1 5⅓-ounce can evaporated milk
 2 tablespoons butter
 1 teaspoon vanilla
 Vanilla ice cream
 Coarsely crushed pretzels
 Whole pretzels

In saucepan combine sugar and cocoa powder. Stir in evaporated milk and 2 tablespoons *water*. Bring mixture to boiling; cook and stir for 3 to 4 minutes. Remove from heat; stir in butter and vanilla. Cover and refrigerate 2 to 24 hours.

Before serving: In saucepan heat fudge sauce. Top 8 individual servings of vanilla ice cream with hot fudge sauce. Sprinkle with crushed pretzels. Garnish each with a whole pretzel. Makes 8 servings.

● **Microwave directions:** Butter sides of a 1½-quart nonmetal casserole. In casserole combine sugar and cocoa powder. Add evaporated milk and 2 tablespoons *water;* stir. Cook in a counter-top microwave oven on high power 3 to 3½ minutes or till boiling, stirring once. Continue to micro-cook 3 to 4 minutes or till of desired consistency, stirring 2 or 3 times. Stir in butter and vanilla. Cover; refrigerate 2 to 24 hours.

Before serving, in a counter-top microwave oven cook sauce in the nonmetal casserole on high power 1 to 2 minutes or till warm. If necessary, beat till smooth. Top ice cream as directed above.

Brunch

Treat your family or friends to a weekend brunch without having to rise at the crack of dawn to start cooking. With our menu you can make all the food the day before to store in the refrigerator, in the freezer, or on the shelf. Then you can sleep late, do the minor last-minute preparation, and enjoy the brunch as if you were a guest.

MENU

Sausage & Caraway Strata

Frosty Fruit Compote

Cinnamon Coffee or Milk

Sausage and Caraway Strata

    6 slices rye bread, toasted
    4 beaten eggs
    2 cups milk
    ½ teaspoon salt
    ½ teaspoon caraway seed
    1 cup shredded American
        cheese (4 ounces)
    ½ cup shredded Swiss cheese
        (2 ounces)
    ½ cup thinly sliced celery
    2 tablespoons finely chopped
        green pepper
    1 5-ounce package small
        smoked sausage links
    ½ cup shredded Swiss cheese
        (2 ounces)

Cut bread in half diagonally. Arrange bread in an 8x8x2-inch baking dish. In bowl combine eggs, milk, salt, and caraway seed. Stir in American cheese, ½ cup Swiss cheese, celery, and green pepper. Pour egg mixture over bread in baking dish. Arrange the sausage atop. Cover and refrigerate 3 to 24 hours.

Before serving: Bake, uncovered, in a 350° oven 45 to 50 minutes. Sprinkle with ½ cup Swiss cheese. Bake 5 minutes more or till a knife inserted near center comes out clean. Let stand 10 minutes. Makes 6 servings.

Frosty Fruit Compote

    2 cups fresh or frozen
        strawberries (loose pack)
    2 cups fresh or frozen peach
        slices (loose pack)
    ¾ cup lemon-lime carbonated
        beverage
    ¼ cup orange liqueur
        Coconut
        Chopped walnuts

Place fresh or frozen strawberries and peaches in a 4- or 5-cup freezer container. (Cut up any large fruits.) Stir together the carbonated beverage and orange liqueur; pour over fruit. Cover, seal, label, and freeze.

Before serving: Let stand at room temperature for 3 hours. Spoon into 6 individual serving dishes. Sprinkle with coconut and walnuts. Makes 6 servings.

Cinnamon Coffee

    ½ cup nonfat dry milk powder
    ½ cup instant coffee crystals
    2 tablespoons sugar
    1 teaspoon ground cinnamon
        Boiling water
        Frozen whipped dessert
        topping, thawed

Combine dry milk powder, instant coffee crystals, sugar, and cinnamon. Store in an airtight container. Makes 1 cup mix.

Before serving: For each serving, place *1 tablespoon* dry coffee mixture into each coffee mug. Add *¾ cup* boiling water; stir till coffee crystals dissolve. Top each with a dollop of dessert topping.

Freezer Dinner in Foil

By planning ahead you can have the ease of convenience foods with the goodness of home cooking. Just prepare several dinners in foil and freeze them with the baking instructions taped to them. Then you or any member of your family can have a complete, wholesome meal simply by removing the package from the freezer and baking it according to the instructions.

MENU

Barbecue-Style
Pork Chops

Cream Cheese
Potatoes

Herbed Carrots

Beverage

Barbecue-Style Pork Chops

    4 pork chops, cut ½ inch thick
    ⅔ cup catsup
    2 tablespoons brown sugar
    2 tablespoons vinegar
    1 tablespoon Worcestershire sauce
    ¼ teaspoon dry mustard
    ¼ teaspoon paprika
    ¼ teaspoon chili powder
      Herbed Carrots (see recipe, at right)
      Cream Cheese Potatoes (see recipe, at right)

Trim excess fat from chops; in skillet cook fat trimmings till 2 tablespoons fat accumulate or use 2 tablespoons cooking oil. Discard trimmings. Cook chops in hot fat or oil for 10 to 15 minutes or till done, turning once. Remove chops; place a chop in the large compartment of each of 4 divided foil trays.

In saucepan combine catsup, brown sugar, vinegar, Worcestershire sauce, dry mustard, paprika, and chili powder. Spoon over chops. Add Herbed Carrots and Cream Cheese Potatoes to trays as directed in recipes at right. Cover with heavy foil. Seal, label, and freeze.

Before serving: Bake frozen dinner, covered, in a 400° oven for 40 to 45 minutes or till heated through. Makes 4 dinners.

Cream Cheese Potatoes

    3 medium potatoes, peeled and quartered
    1 3-ounce package cream cheese with chives
    1 tablespoon butter *or* margarine
      Milk

In covered saucepan cook potatoes in enough boiling salted water to cover for 20 to 25 minutes or till done. Drain off water; mash potatoes.

Add cream cheese and butter or margarine to potatoes, stirring till cream cheese is melted. Beat in enough milk (about 2 tablespoons) to make potatoes a stiff consistency. Season to taste with salt and pepper. Spoon some mashed potato mixture into a small compartment of each of 4 divided foil trays. Cook as directed in Barbecue-Style Pork Chops.

Herbed Carrots

    2 cups frozen crinkle-cut sliced carrots
    3 tablespoons butter *or* margarine, melted
    ⅛ teaspoon dried basil, crushed
    ½ teaspoon lemon juice

Spoon ½ cup frozen carrots into a small compartment of each of 4 divided foil trays. Combine melted butter or margarine, basil, and lemon juice; spoon over carrots. Cook as directed in Barbecue-Style Pork Chops.

Main Dishes

The main dish doesn't have to be the most time-consuming part of preparing a meal. With this chapter you can plan ahead and prepare a main dish when your schedule permits.

To use your time efficiently, turn to the four pages of Double-Duty Recipes. Each of these starts with a basic mixture that is used to prepare three main dishes at once.

The remainder of the chapter is divided into refrigerator main dishes and freezer main dishes.

When you want to cook for tomorrow's dinner, choose a refrigerator main dish. Or, turn to the freezer main dish recipes to prepare foods that can be served a week or even a month later.

Recipes are prepared ahead without sacrificing taste. Choose from main dish salads, stews, stratas, casseroles, and sandwiches.

Recipes with last-minute baking require little attention from the cook. Others are served right from the refrigerator.

Cheese Manicotti (see recipe, page 44)
Freezer Stuffed Peppers (see recipe, page 49)
Gazpacho-Topped Chilled Meat Loaf (see recipe, page 29)
Turkey Pies (see recipe, page 25)

Double-Duty Recipes

Basic Meat Mixture

- 3 pounds lean boneless pork, cut into bite-size strips
- 1½ cups chopped onion
- 1 cup chopped green pepper
- 3 tablespoons cooking oil

In large skillet cook *half* the cut up pork, the chopped onion, and chopped green pepper in cooking oil till the meat is browned and vegetables are tender. Remove from skillet. Cook the remaining pork till browned.

Return all to skillet and stir to mix. Divide mixture into three 2½-cup portions to use in preparing the following recipes: Stroganoff-Style Pork, Meat Turnovers, and Hearty Meat Soup.

1

Stroganoff-Style Pork

- 1 2½-cup portion Basic Meat Mixture
- 1 10½-ounce can condensed beef broth
- 1 3-ounce can sliced mushrooms, drained
- 2 tablespoons catsup
- ½ teaspoon Worcestershire sauce
- 1 cup dairy sour cream
- 3 tablespoons all-purpose flour
  Hot cooked noodles

Combine the Basic Meat Mixture, broth, mushrooms, catsup, and Worcestershire sauce; heat to boiling. Combine sour cream and flour. Gradually blend some meat mixture into sour cream; return to skillet. Cook and stir till thick and bubbly. Turn into 5-cup container. Cover; refrigerate for 3 to 24 hours.

Before serving: Return to skillet; heat through. Serve over hot cooked noodles. Sprinkle with snipped parsley, if desired. Makes 4 to 6 servings.

2

Meat Turnovers   *used crescent rolls*

- 2 cups all-purpose flour
- 2 tablespoons grated Parmesan cheese
- ⅔ cup shortening
- 5 to 7 tablespoons cold water
- ½ cup plain yogurt
- 2 teaspoons all-purpose flour
- ½ teaspoon ground sage

Basic Ground Meat Mixture

- 3 pounds ground beef *or* ground pork
- 1 cup chopped onion
- ½ cup chopped green pepper
- 3 cloves garlic, minced
- 1 16-ounce can tomatoes
- 1 18-ounce can tomato paste
- 2 teaspoons sugar

Cook meat, onion, green pepper, and garlic till meat is browned. Drain off fat. Cut up tomatoes. Add *undrained* tomatoes, tomato paste, sugar, 1½ teaspoons *salt*, and ¼ teaspoon *pepper*. Cover; simmer about 15 minutes. Divide mixture into three 2½-cup portions for use in the following recipes: Spicy Chili, Corn Bread Tacos, and Layered Meat Pie.

1

Spicy Chili

- 1 2½-cup portion Basic Ground Meat Mixture
- 1 15½-ounce can red kidney beans
- 2 to 3 teaspoons chili powder
- ½ teaspoon dry mustard
- 1 12-ounce can beer
- 1 8¼-ounce can sliced carrots

In a bowl stir together the Basic Ground Meat Mixture, *undrained* kidney beans, chili powder, and dry mustard. Spoon the mixture into a 5- or 6-cup freezer container. Cover, seal, label, and freeze.

Before serving: In saucepan combine the frozen mixture and the can of beer. Cover and cook over medium-low heat about 35 minutes, breaking apart frozen mixture with a fork. Cover and cook 5 minutes more. Stir in the *undrained* carrots. Cook mixture till heated through. Makes 6 servings.

2

Corn Bread Tacos

- 1 2½-cup portion Basic Ground Meat Mixture
- 1 4-ounce can green chili peppers, rinsed, seeded, and chopped
- 1 teaspoon chili powder
- 1 teaspoon Worcestershire sauce
  Several dashes bottled hot pepper sauce

1 2½-cup portion Basic Meat
  Mixture
1 5-ounce jar American cheese
  spread with pimiento

Combine the 2 cups flour and Parmesan cheese. Cut in shortening till mixture resembles small peas. Sprinkle *1 tablespoon* water over part of mixture; toss. Repeat with remaining water till all is moistened; form into a ball.

For filling, combine yogurt, 2 teaspoons flour, sage, and ½ teaspoon *salt.* Stir in meat mixture. Divide dough into 6 portions. Roll *each* portion into a 10x5-inch rectangle. Spread *each* with cheese to ½ inch of edges. Spoon about ⅔ cup filling on half of *each* rectangle. Moisten pastry edges with water; fold over filling to form a square. Seal edges. Cut slits in top.

Place on baking sheet. Cover with plastic wrap; freeze. Wrap, seal, label, and freeze.

Before serving: Place frozen turnovers on a baking sheet. Brush with milk, if desired. Bake in a 375° oven about 60 minutes or till done. Makes 6 servings.

3

Hearty Meat Soup

1 2½-cup portion Basic Meat
  Mixture
1 8-ounce can red kidney
  beans
1 7½-ounce can tomatoes, cut
  up
1 7-ounce can whole kernel
  corn
½ cup ditali *or* elbow macaroni

¼ cup dry red wine
2 teaspoons instant beef
  bouillon granules
½ teaspoon dried basil, crushed
¼ teaspoon ground red pepper
  Grated Parmesan cheese

Combine Basic Meat Mixture, *undrained* kidney beans, *undrained* tomatoes, *undrained* corn, the pasta, red wine, bouillon granules, basil, red pepper, and 1⅔ cups *water.* Bring to boiling; cover and simmer about 20 minutes. Cool slightly. Spoon into 6-cup freezer container. Cover, seal, label, and freeze.

Before serving: In covered saucepan heat frozen mixture with ¼ cup *water* about 35 minutes, breaking apart mixture with a fork. Heat through. Serve with Parmesan cheese. Serves 4 or 5.

---

6 frozen corn muffins *or*
  cornbread squares
  Shredded lettuce
  Shredded American cheese
  Chopped tomato

Combine the Basic Ground Meat Mixture, chopped green chilies, chili powder, Worcestershire sauce, and bottled hot pepper sauce. Spoon mixture into 4-cup freezer container. Cover, seal, label, and freeze.

Before serving: In medium saucepan combine frozen meat mixture and ¼ cup *water.* Cook, covered, over medium-low heat about 35 minutes or till thawed, breaking apart mixture with a fork. Cover; cook till heated through. Meanwhile, heat muffins according to package directions. (Or, wrap

cornbread in foil; bake in a 350° oven for 5 to 10 minutes.)

Halve muffins or cornbread horizontally; place on individual serving plates. Spoon meat mixture over. Top with lettuce, cheese, and tomato. Makes 6 servings.

3

Layered Meat Pie

6 ounces fine noodles
2 tablespoons butter
2 beaten eggs
⅓ cup grated Parmesan cheese
2 tablespoons snipped parsley
½ cup shredded provolone
  cheese (2 ounces)
1 teaspoon dried basil, crushed
1 2½-cup portion Basic Ground
  Meat Mixture

½ cup shredded provolone
  cheese (2 ounces)

Cook noodles in a large amount of boiling salted water for 10 to 12 minutes or just till tender; drain. Stir butter into hot noodles; stir in beaten eggs, Parmesan cheese, and parsley. Spoon noodle mixture into a greased 10-inch pie plate, forming a crust. Sprinkle with ½ cup shredded provolone cheese.

Stir basil into the Basic Ground Meat Mixture. Turn meat mixture into noodle crust. Cover and refrigerate for 3 to 24 hours.

Before serving: Cover edges of pie with foil. Bake in a 350° oven for 45 to 50 minutes. Sprinkle with ½ cup shredded provolone cheese; bake 5 minutes more or till cheese melts. Let stand 10 minutes before serving. Makes 6 servings.

Double-Duty Recipes

Basic Turkey Mixture

1 2½-pound frozen boneless turkey roast
1 cup milk
1 tablespoon cornstarch
1 10¾-ounce can *each* condensed cream of celery *and* cream of mushroom soup
2 3-ounce packages cream cheese with chives, cut up
1 6-ounce can sliced mushrooms, drained

Bake roast according to package directions. Cool; cut into ½-inch cubes. Combine milk and cornstarch; add soups. Cook and stir till bubbly; continue 2 minutes more. Stir in cream cheese. Stir in mushrooms and turkey. Divide into three 2⅔-cup portions to use in making the recipes at the right.

1

Swiss Turkey Crepes

1 10-ounce package frozen cut broccoli
2 tablespoons dry white wine
1 2⅔-cup portion Basic Turkey Mixture
12 Make-Ahead Crepes
1 cup shredded Swiss cheese
½ cup shredded cheddar cheese

Cook broccoli according to package directions; drain. Stir broccoli and wine into turkey mixture.

Spoon ⅓ *cup* mixture onto unbrowned side of each crepe. Fold opposite sides to overlap atop. Place seam side down in 13x9x2-inch baking dish. Cover; refrigerate for 3 to 24 hours.

Before serving: Bake crepes, covered, in 375° oven about 30 minutes. Combine cheeses; sprinkle atop. Bake 3 minutes more. Serves 6.

Make-Ahead Crepes: Mix 1½ cups *milk,* 1 cup all-purpose *flour,* 2 *eggs,* 1 tablespoon *cooking oil,* and ¼ teaspoon *salt;* beat well. Heat greased 6-inch skillet. Remove from heat; add 2 *tablespoons* batter. Tilt to spread batter. Return to heat; brown on one side. Invert over paper toweling, removing crepe. Repeat with remaining batter, greasing skillet occasionally. Makes 16 to 18.

To freeze, stack crepes alternating each with 2 layers of waxed paper. Overwrap with moisture-vaporproof bag. Place in freezer container. Freeze. Thaw at room temperature 1 hour before using.

Basic Seafood Mixture

2 pounds fresh *or* frozen fish fillets
1 15-ounce can tomato sauce
1 12-ounce can tomato paste
3 tablespoons cooking oil
1½ teaspoons sugar
1 pound fresh *or* frozen shelled shrimp, halved

If frozen, let fish stand at room temperature 20 minutes. Cut fish into 1-inch pieces. Stir together the tomato sauce, tomato paste, cooking oil, and sugar. Gently stir in the fish pieces and halved shrimp. Divide mixture into three 3½-cup portions for use in the following recipes: Seafood Sauce with Spaghetti, Seafood with Rice, and Seafood-Stuffed Peppers.

1

Seafood Sauce with Spaghetti

½ cup chopped green pepper
1 clove garlic, minced
1 tablespoon cooking oil
1 3½-cup portion Basic Seafood Mixture
¼ cup dry white *or* red wine
1 3-ounce can sliced mushrooms, drained
2 tablespoons snipped parsley
½ teaspoon dried oregano, crushed
½ teaspoon dried basil, crushed
Hot cooked spaghetti

In saucepan cook green pepper and garlic in hot oil till tender. Remove from heat. Stir in Basic Seafood Mixture, dry white or red wine, sliced mushrooms, snipped parsley, oregano, and basil. Turn the seafood sauce mixture into a 4-cup freezer container. Cover, seal, label, and freeze.

Before serving: In saucepan place frozen seafood mixture; heat through. Serve over hot cooked spaghetti. Pass Parmesan cheese, if desired. Makes 4 servings.

2

Seafood with Rice

½ cup sliced celery
¼ cup chopped onion
1 clove garlic, minced
2 tablespoons butter *or* margarine

2

Turkey Chowder

1 2⅔-cup portion Basic Turkey
    Mixture
1 16-ounce can stewed
    tomatoes
¼ teaspoon dried rosemary,
    crushed
¼ teaspoon garlic salt

Combine all ingredients above and
⅛ teaspoon *pepper.* Spoon into 6-
cup freezer container. Cover, seal,
label, and freeze.

Before serving: In covered
saucepan heat frozen chowder
and ½ cup *water* about 35 minutes
or till thawed, breaking apart mixture with a fork. Heat just to boiling.
Makes 4 servings.

3

Turkey Pies

Pictured on pages 20 and 21 —

1 10-ounce package frozen
    peas and carrots
1 2⅔-cup portion Basic Turkey
    Mixture
½ cup all-purpose flour
½ cup whole wheat flour
2 tablespoons finely chopped
    sunflower nuts
⅓ cup shortening

In colander run hot water over frozen vegetables till partially thawed,
if necessary to separate. Stir vegetables into the Basic Turkey Mixture. Spoon mixture into four 12-
ounce casseroles. In mixing bowl
stir together the all-purpose flour,
whole wheat flour, sunflower nuts,
and dash *salt.* Cut in shortening till
mixture resembles small peas.
Sprinkle 1 tablespoon *cold water*
over part of mixture; gently toss
with fork. Push to side of bowl. Repeat, using 2 to 4 tablespoons *cold
water,* till all is moistened. Divide
dough into 4 portions. On floured
surface roll each portion to fit casserole. Cut out design in center of
dough with cookie cutter. Place
dough atop casseroles; flute edges.
Cover each casserole with moisture-vaporproof wrap. Seal, label,
and freeze.

Before serving: Brush tops with
milk, if desired. Bake in 350° oven
about 60 minutes. Let stand 10
minutes before serving. Serves 4.

---

1 7½-ounce can tomatoes, cut
    up
½ teaspoon dried thyme,
    crushed
    Few dashes bottled hot
    pepper sauce
1 3½-cup portion Basic
    Seafood Mixture
¼ cup water
    Hot cooked rice

Cook celery, onion, and garlic in
butter or margarine till tender. Remove from heat. Stir in *undrained*
tomatoes, thyme, and hot pepper
sauce. Stir in Basic Seafood Mixture. Turn into a 4-cup freezer container. Cover, seal, label, and freeze.

Before serving: Combine frozen mixture and water; heat
through. Spoon into serving bowls.
Top each with a mound of hot
cooked rice. Serves 4.

3

Seafood-Stuffed Peppers

4 large green peppers
1 3½-cup portion Basic
    Seafood Mixture
½ cup cooked rice
1 teaspoon dried basil, crushed
1 teaspoon Worcestershire
    sauce
½ cup shredded mozzarella
    cheese (2 ounces)
¼ cup shredded mozzarella
    cheese (1 ounce)

Using a knife, cut off tops of green
peppers; remove seeds and mem-
brane. In saucepan precook peppers in boiling salted water for 5
minutes; invert to drain. (For crisp

peppers, omit precooking.)
    Combine the Basic Seafood Mix-
ture, cooked rice, crushed dried
basil, Worcestershire sauce, and
the ½ cup shredded mozzarella
cheese. Spoon into pepper shells.
Stand filled peppers upright in a
10x6x2-inch baking dish. Cover
and refrigerate for 2 to 24 hours.

Before serving: Bake, uncovered, in a 350° oven about 40 minutes or till heated through. Sprinkle
the ¼ cup shredded mozzarella
cheese atop peppers. Return to
oven; bake about 3 minutes more
or till mozzarella cheese melts.
Makes 4 servings.

Main Dishes to Refrigerate

Meats

Marinated Flank Steak

1 1- to 1¼-pound flank steak
¼ cup cooking oil
3 tablespoons soy sauce
1 tablespoon dry red wine
1 tablespoon instant coffee
      crystals
1 clove garlic, minced
¼ teaspoon pepper
      Few dashes bottled hot
      pepper sauce

Score steak diagonally at 1-inch intervals on both sides. Place steak in a shallow baking dish. Combine cooking oil, soy sauce, dry red wine, instant coffee crystals, minced garlic, pepper, and the hot pepper sauce. Stir mixture till coffee crystals dissolve. Pour mixture over steak. Cover and refrigerate for 3 to 24 hours, turning steak occasionally.

Before serving: Remove steak from marinade, reserving marinade. Place steak on rack of unheated broiler pan. Broil 3 inches from heat for 4 to 5 minutes. Turn steak; brush with marinade. Broil for 4 to 5 minutes more for medium-rare doneness. (Or, grill marinated steak over medium-hot coals for 6 to 8 minutes. Turn; brush with marinade. Grill 6 to 8 minutes more for medium-rare doneness.)

To serve, brush broiled steak with marinade and carve into very thin slices diagonally across the grain. Makes 4 or 5 servings.

Beef and Green Chili Tortillas

1 pound beef flank steak
½ cup hot mustard
8 to 12 flour tortillas
2 medium tomatoes
1 medium red onion
1 4-ounce can green chili
      peppers, rinsed, seeded,
      and chopped

Score meat diagonally at 1-inch intervals on both sides. Spread *half* the mustard on each side of steak. Place in shallow baking dish. Cover and refrigerate for 3 to 24 hours.

To make sauce, finely chop tomatoes and onion. In mixing bowl combine tomatoes, onion, and chili peppers. Cover and refrigerate.

Before serving: Place steak on rack of unheated broiler pan. Broil 3 inches from heat for 4 to 5 minutes. Sprinkle with salt and pepper. Turn steak; broil 4 to 5 minutes more for medium-rare doneness. Sprinkle with salt and pepper.

Warm tortillas in the oven according to package directions. Meanwhile, cut steak into thin slices diagonally across the grain. Place several slices atop each tortilla. Spoon on sauce. Roll up. Makes 4 to 6 servings.

Oven-Going Foods

Cover baking dishes with foil or a lid before refrigerating to avoid rewrapping foods that are covered and baked before serving.

Pineapple-Beef Salad

½ cup sliced carrots
⅓ cup salad oil
¼ cup white wine vinegar
¼ cup sliced green onion
2 tablespoons snipped parsley
1 tablespoon sugar
1 teaspoon dry mustard
¼ teaspoon salt
¼ teaspoon dried tarragon,
      crushed
2 cups cooked beef, cut into
      julienne strips
½ cup green pepper strips
2 cups torn mixed salad greens
1 15½-ounce can pineapple
      chunks, drained

In saucepan cook carrots in a small amount of boiling salted water for 5 to 10 minutes or till crisp-tender; drain and set aside. For marinade, in screw-top jar combine salad oil, white wine vinegar, sliced green onion, snipped parsley, sugar, dry mustard, salt, and tarragon; shake well.

In a small bowl sprinkle cooked beef with a little salt and pepper. Add sliced carrots and green pepper strips. Pour marinade over beef mixture. Cover and refrigerate for 3 to 24 hours, stirring occasionally.

Before serving: Drain beef and vegetables, reserving marinade. Arrange torn mixed greens in salad bowl. Top with the drained beef mixture and pineapple chunks; drizzle with reserved marinade. Toss lightly. Makes 4 servings.

Meats

Portuguese Beef Stew

  3 pounds beef stew meat, cut
     into 1-inch cubes
  2 tablespoons cooking oil
  2 cups water
  1 8-ounce can tomato sauce
  2 bay leaves
  2 tablespoons vinegar
  2 teaspoons salt
  1 teaspoon garlic powder
  ½ to 1 teaspoon crushed red
     pepper
  ½ teaspoon ground cinnamon
  ½ teaspoon ground allspice
  5 medium potatoes, peeled and
     cut into 1-inch pieces
  4 medium carrots, cut into ½-
     inch pieces
  ½ cup cold water
  3 tablespoons cornstarch

In Dutch oven quickly cook meat, half at a time, in hot oil till browned. Return all meat to pan. Stir in the 2 cups water, the tomato sauce, bay leaves, vinegar, salt, garlic powder, crushed red pepper, cinnamon, and allspice. Simmer, covered, for 1 hour.

Add potatoes and carrots; simmer, covered, 30 to 40 minutes more. Combine ½ cup cold water and cornstarch. Stir into stew. Cook and stir till thickened and bubbly. Cook and stir 1 to 2 minutes more. Remove bay leaves. Turn into 3-quart casserole. Cover and refrigerate for 3 to 24 hours.

Before serving: Bake, covered, in a 375° oven about 1 hour or till heated through, stirring occasionally. Makes 8 servings.

Old-Fashioned Corned Tongue

  1 cup pickling salt
  8 cups water
  2 tablespoons sugar
  1 tablespoon mixed pickling
     spice
  1 teaspoon paprika
  ½ teaspoon saltpeter
     (potassium nitrate)
     (optional)
  ½ teaspoon freshly ground
     pepper
  ¼ teaspoon ground cloves
  3 bay leaves
  1 3- to 4-pound beef tongue
  ¼ cup chopped onion
  2 cloves garlic
  1 medium onion, sliced
  1 teaspoon whole black pepper
  4 bay leaves

In large saucepan dissolve salt in water. Add sugar, pickling spice, paprika, saltpeter, ground pepper, cloves, and 3 bay leaves. Bring to boiling; boil 5 minutes. Remove from heat. Cool.

Place tongue in a crock. Add chopped onion and garlic. Cover with salt mixture. Place a plate atop meat. Cover with clear plastic wrap. Place a heavy weight, such as a water-filled jar, atop covered plate. Refrigerate 3 weeks, turning meat once a week.

Before serving: Remove tongue from brine; place in a large Dutch oven or kettle. Cover tongue with hot water. Add sliced onion, whole pepper, and 4 bay leaves. Cover; simmer 3 to 4 hours (1 hour per pound) or till meat is tender. Remove meat; cool slightly. Cut off bones and gristle. Slit skin on underside from large end to tip; peel off. Slice meat diagonally. Makes 8 to 10 servings.

Teriyaki Roast Beef

  ½ cup dry sherry
  ¼ cup soy sauce
  2 tablespoons dry onion
     soup mix
  2 tablespoons brown sugar
  1 3-pound beef eye round roast
  2 tablespoons water

In a small bowl stir together the dry sherry, soy sauce, the onion soup mix, and brown sugar. Place beef in plastic bag; set in a deep bowl or a shallow baking dish. Pour marinade mixture over meat. Close bag or cover dish. Refrigerate for 8 to 24 hours, turning bag or spooning marinade over meat occasionally to coat evenly.

Before serving: Drain meat, reserving marinade. Place on rack in roasting pan. Bake in a 325° oven about 1½ hours or till done; baste occasionally with *half* of the marinade. In saucepan combine remaining marinade and the water; bring to boiling. Slice cooked meat; spoon hot marinade mixture over. Makes 8 servings.

Main Dishes to Refrigerate

Meats

Oriental Beef Bake

1 pound ground beef *or* ground pork
½ cup chopped green pepper
1 clove garlic, minced
½ cup cold water
3 tablespoons soy sauce
3 tablespoons cornstarch
½ teaspoon ground ginger
1 cup loose pack frozen broccoli, cauliflower, and carrot
1 cup water
½ cup quick-cooking rice
⅓ cup sliced water chestnuts

In skillet cook ground beef or ground pork, green pepper, and garlic till meat is browned and green pepper is tender. Drain off fat. Combine ½ cup cold water, soy sauce, cornstarch, and ginger; stir into meat. Cook and stir till thickened and bubbly. Stir in frozen mixed vegetables, the 1 cup water, quick-cooking rice, and sliced water chestnuts.

Turn mixture into a 1½-quart casserole. Cover and refrigerate for 3 to 24 hours.

Before serving: Bake, covered, in a 350° oven about 40 minutes or till done, stirring twice. Makes 4 servings.

Festive Pork Roast (see recipe, page 30)
Overnight Sausage Salad (see recipe, page 33)
Crepes Saltimbocca

Crepes Saltimbocca

½ pound ground beef
1 medium onion, chopped (½ cup)
2 tablespoons grated Parmesan cheese
½ teaspoon ground sage
2 2½- *or* 3-ounce packages thinly sliced smoked ham
12 Make-Ahead Crepes (see recipe, page 25)
1 6-ounce package mozzarella cheese slices (4 long slices)
2 tablespoons milk
½ cup dairy sour cream
  Chopped green onion (optional)

Cook ground beef and onion till meat is browned. Drain well. Stir in Parmesan cheese and sage. Divide ham slices among crepes, arranging them on the unbrowned side. Cut cheese slices crosswise into thirds. Place one piece atop ham on each crepe. Spoon about *2 tablespoons* beef mixture down the center of each. Fold two opposite sides of crepes so they overlap atop filling. Place, seam side down, in a greased 13x9x2-inch baking dish. Cover and refrigerate for 3 to 24 hours.

Before serving: Bake, covered, in 375° oven about 35 minutes. Stir milk into sour cream. Stir in chopped green onion, if desired; dollop atop crepes. Makes 6 servings.

Gazpacho-Topped Chilled Meat Loaf

Pictured on pages 20 and 21 —

2 beaten eggs
½ cup chili sauce
⅓ cup fine dry bread crumbs
1 3-ounce can chopped mushrooms, drained
1 tablespoon prepared horseradish
1½ teaspoons salt
1 teaspoon dried thyme, crushed
⅛ teaspoon pepper
1 pound ground beef
1 pound ground pork
  Cooked asparagus spears (optional)
  Gazpacho Relish

In mixing bowl combine eggs, chili sauce, bread crumbs, mushrooms, horseradish, salt, thyme, and pepper. Add ground beef and ground pork; mix well. Shape meat mixture into an 8x4-inch loaf. Place in shallow baking pan. Bake in 350° oven for 1½ hours. Drain off fat; cool. Cover and refrigerate for 3 to 24 hours. Prepare Gazpacho Relish.

Before serving: Place on serving platter. Garnish with asparagus spears, if desired. Top with Gazpacho Relish. Makes 8 servings.

Gazpacho Relish: Combine 3 medium *tomatoes,* peeled and finely chopped (2 cups), ½ cup finely chopped *green pepper,* ⅓ cup *vinegar,* ¼ cup finely chopped *onion,* 1 tablespoon *sugar,* ¾ teaspoon *celery salt,* ½ teaspoon *mustard seed,* ¼ teaspoon *salt,* and dash *pepper.* Cover and chill.

29

Meats

Festive Pork Roast

Pictured on page 28 —

- ¾ cup dry red wine
- ⅓ cup packed brown sugar
- ¼ cup vinegar
- ¼ cup catsup
- ¼ cup water
- 2 tablespoons cooking oil
- 1 tablespoon soy sauce
- 1 clove garlic, minced
- 1 teaspoon curry powder
- ½ teaspoon ground ginger
- ¼ teaspoon pepper
- 1 5-pound boneless rolled pork roast
- 2 teaspoons cornstarch

For marinade, combine wine, brown sugar, vinegar, catsup, water, cooking oil, soy sauce, garlic, curry powder, ginger, and pepper. Place meat in plastic bag; set in shallow baking dish. Pour marinade over meat; close bag. Refrigerate for 6 to 24 hours, turning several times.

Before serving: Drain meat, reserving 1¼ cups marinade. Place meat on rack in shallow roasting pan. Roast in 325° oven for 2¼ to 2¾ hours or till meat thermometer registers 170°

Meanwhile, in saucepan combine reserved marinade and cornstarch; cook and stir till thickened and bubbly. Cook and stir 1 to 2 minutes more. Brush roast frequently with this mixture during last 15 minutes of cooking.

Place roast on serving platter. Garnish with kumquats, green grapes, and curly endive, if desired. Reheat remaining sauce and pass with meat. Makes 15 servings.

Pork and Zucchini Casserole

- 1½ pounds zucchini, sliced ¾ inch thick
- 1 pound boneless pork, thinly sliced into bite-size strips
- ¼ cup chopped onion
- 2 tablespoons cooking oil
- 1 10¾-ounce can condensed cream of celery soup
- 1 cup dairy sour cream
- ½ cup shredded carrot
- ¼ cup butter *or* margarine
- 2 cups herb-seasoned stuffing mix

In a saucepan cook sliced zucchini in boiling salted water about 5 minutes or just till crisp-tender. Drain and set aside. In a large skillet cook pork and onion in hot cooking oil till pork is browned and onion is tender. Drain off fat.

Stir cooked zucchini, cream of celery soup, sour cream, and the shredded carrot into meat. Melt butter or margarine; sprinkle over stuffing mix, tossing well. Spread *half* the stuffing mixture into a 12x7½x2-inch baking dish. Spoon the pork-zucchini mixture atop. Sprinkle with remaining stuffing mixture. Cover and refrigerate for 3 to 24 hours.

Before serving: Bake, uncovered, in a 350° oven for 35 to 40 minutes or till casserole is heated through. Makes 6 servings.

Apple- and Orange-Stuffed Pork Chops

- 6 pork loin rib chops, cut 1½ inches thick
- ½ cup chopped celery
- 1 medium apple, chopped (½ cup)
- 2 tablespoons butter *or* margarine
- 1 beaten egg
- 1½ cups toasted raisin bread cubes (2½ slices bread)
- ½ teaspoon finely shredded orange peel
- 1 orange, peeled, sectioned, and chopped (⅓ cup)
- ¼ teaspoon salt
- ⅛ teaspoon ground cinnamon
- 1 tablespoon cooking oil

Cut a pocket in each chop. Season cavity with a little salt and pepper. In small saucepan cook celery and apple in butter or margarine till tender but not brown. Combine egg, bread cubes, orange peel, chopped orange, salt, and cinnamon. Pour cooked celery and apple over bread cube mixture; toss lightly. Spoon about ⅓ cup of the stuffing mixture into each pork chop. Securely fasten pocket opening with wooden picks.

In large skillet brown chops slowly in hot cooking oil, 3 at a time, for 10 to 15 minutes. Place chops in 13x9x2-inch baking dish. Cover and refrigerate for 3 to 24 hours.

Before serving: Bake, covered, in a 350° oven for 65 to 70 minutes or till meat is tender. Remove the picks; garnish with orange slices, if desired. Makes 6 servings.

Meats

Ham Risotto

¼ cup chopped onion
¼ cup chopped green pepper
1 tablespoon butter *or* margarine
2½ cups water
2 cups diced fully cooked ham
1 cup long grain rice
⅓ cup sliced celery
2 teaspoons instant chicken bouillon granules
Dash pepper
1 small tomato, peeled, seeded, and chopped
½ cup quartered fresh mushrooms
½ teaspoon dried basil, crushed
¼ teaspoon dried tarragon, crushed
⅛ teaspoon celery seed

In saucepan cook the chopped onion and green pepper in butter or margarine till tender but not brown. Stir in the water, diced ham, uncooked rice, sliced celery, chicken bouillon granules, and pepper. Stir in the tomato, fresh mushrooms, basil, tarragon, and celery seed. Turn mixture into 10x6x2-inch baking dish. Cover and refrigerate for 3 to 24 hours.

Before serving: Bake, covered, in a 350° oven for 1¼ hours. Gently stir mixture. Return to oven. Bake about 15 minutes more or till the rice is done. Makes 4 to 6 servings.

Ham and Cheese Salad

2 teaspoons instant chicken bouillon granules
1 cup long grain rice
1 cup frozen peas
1½ cups diced fully cooked ham
3 ounces cheddar cheese, cubed
2 tablespoons sliced green onion
½ cup green goddess salad dressing
¼ cup milk
Lettuce leaves
Sliced pitted ripe olives

In saucepan combine bouillon granules and 2 cups *water.* Add uncooked rice and cook according to package directions. Chill.

In colander run hot water over peas till thawed. In bowl combine the cooked rice, peas, diced ham, cubed cheese, and green onion. Stir together the dressing and milk. Add to salad; toss well. Cover and refrigerate for 3 to 24 hours.

Before serving: Toss ham-rice mixture. Serve atop lettuce leaves. Garnish with sliced pitted ripe olives. Makes 4 servings.

Ham-Stuffed Sweet Potatoes

4 large sweet potatoes
2 cups diced fully cooked ham
⅓ cup cranberry-orange relish
¼ cup light raisins
2 tablespoons brown sugar
¼ teaspoon salt
¼ cup butter *or* margarine, softened

Scrub sweet potatoes with brush. Prick with fork. Bake in a 425° oven about 40 minutes or till done. Cut slice from top of each baked sweet potato. Scoop out inside, leaving ½-inch shell; chop the cooked potato.

Combine diced ham, cranberry-orange relish, raisins, brown sugar, salt, and butter or margarine. Fold in chopped potato. Spoon mixture into potato shells. Place in shallow baking dish. Cover and refrigerate for 3 to 24 hours.

Before serving: Bake potatoes, uncovered, in 350° oven about 45 minutes or till heated through. Makes 4 servings.

Easy Ham Strata

8 French bread slices, cut ½ inch thick
Prepared mustard
4 slices Swiss cheese (4 ounces)
1½ cups diced fully cooked ham
4 beaten eggs
2 cups milk

Spread 4 slices of bread with mustard. Place remaining 4 slices in an 8x8x2-inch baking dish. Top each with a slice of Swiss cheese and ¼ of the ham. Cover with remaining bread, mustard side down. Combine eggs and milk; gradually pour over bread. Cover and refrigerate for 3 to 24 hours.

Before serving: Uncover and bake in 325° oven 50 to 60 minutes or till set. (Center may seem unset.) Let stand 10 minutes before serving. Makes 4 servings.

Meats

Lamb and Carrot Kebabs

    4 medium carrots, bias-sliced
        into ½-inch lengths
    1 pound boneless lamb, cut
        into 1-inch pieces
    1 small zucchini, sliced ½ inch
        thick
    8 whole fresh mushrooms
    ¼ cup soy sauce
    ¼ cup honey
    2 tablespoons thinly sliced
        green onion
    2 tablespoons dry sherry
    ¼ teaspoon ground ginger

In covered saucepan cook carrots in a small amount of boiling salted water for 5 to 7 minutes or just till tender; drain well. Place carrots, lamb, zucchini, and mushrooms in plastic bag. Combine soy sauce, honey, green onion, sherry, and ginger; pour over lamb and vegetables. Close bag and place in a bowl or shallow baking dish. Refrigerate for 3 to 24 hours, turning bag occasionally to distribute the marinade.

Before serving: Drain vegetables and lamb, reserving marinade. Thread vegetables and lamb alternately on 4 skewers. Brush with marinade. Place on rack of unheated broiler pan. Broil 4 inches from heat for 10 to 12 minutes or till done; turn and brush with marinade occasionally. (Or, grill over *hot* coals for 10 to 12 minutes; turn and brush with marinade occasionally.) Makes 4 servings.

Lamb Chops with Mustard Sauce

    4 lamb leg sirloin chops, cut
        ¾ inch thick
    1 tablespoon cooking oil
    ¼ cup chopped onion
    2 tablespoons cornstarch
    1 tablespoon dry mustard
    1 teaspoon instant beef
        bouillon granules
    ¼ teaspoon dried oregano,
        crushed
    1 cup milk
    1 8-ounce can stewed
        tomatoes
    1 tablespoon vinegar
      Hot cooked rice

In skillet brown chops in hot oil about 5 minutes per side. Season with salt and pepper. Remove chops, reserving drippings.

Cook onion in reserved drippings till tender but not brown. Stir in cornstarch, dry mustard, bouillon granules, and oregano. Add milk all at once. Cook and stir till thickened and bubbly. Remove from heat. Stir in *undrained* tomatoes and vinegar; set aside.

Arrange chops in an 8x8x2-inch baking dish. Spoon sauce over the chops. Cover and refrigerate for 2 to 24 hours.

Before serving: Bake, covered, in a 350° oven about 60 minutes or till chops are tender. Serve atop rice. Makes 4 servings.

Sausage Lasagna

    ¾ pound bulk Italian sausage
    ¼ cup finely chopped onion
    ¼ cup finely chopped celery
    ¼ cup finely chopped carrot
    1 clove garlic, minced
    1 7½-ounce can tomatoes,
        cut up
    1 6-ounce can tomato paste
    ¼ cup dry red wine
    1 teaspoon dried basil, crushed
    ⅛ teaspoon pepper
 1½ cups ricotta *or* cream-style
        cottage cheese
    ¼ cup grated Parmesan cheese
    2 beaten eggs
    2 tablespoons snipped parsley
    ⅛ teaspoon pepper
    6 lasagna noodles, cooked and
        drained
    6 ounces mozzarella cheese,
        thinly sliced

In skillet cook sausage, onion, celery, carrot, and garlic till meat is browned. Drain off fat. Stir in *undrained* tomatoes, tomato paste, dry red wine, basil, and ⅛ teaspoon pepper. Simmer, covered, about 15 minutes, stirring occasionally.

Combine ricotta or cream-style cottage cheese, the Parmesan cheese, eggs, parsley, and ⅛ teaspoon pepper. Place *half* the lasagna noodles in a 10x6x2-inch baking dish. Spread with *half* the cheese mixture; top with *half* the mozzarella cheese, then *half* the meat sauce. Repeat layers. Cover and refrigerate for 3 to 24 hours.

Before serving: Bake, covered, in a 375° oven for 45 minutes. Uncover; bake 15 minutes more. Let stand 10 minutes. Serves 6.

Meats

Overnight Sausage Salad

Pictured on page 28 —

6 cups torn iceberg lettuce
¾ cup frozen peas
1 4-ounce package sliced
    pepperoni
¾ cup shredded cheddar
    cheese
1 15-ounce can garbanzo
    beans, drained
¼ cup green goddess salad
    dressing
¼ cup mayonnaise

In salad bowl layer *half* the lettuce, all the frozen peas, pepperoni, cheese, and garbanzo beans. Top with remaining lettuce. Combine green goddess dressing and mayonnaise; spread over top, sealing to edge of bowl. Cover and refrigerate for 3 to 24 hours.

Before serving: Garnish with sliced green pepper, if desired. Toss well. Makes 4 servings.

Cheesy Noodle Casserole

4 ounces medium noodles
1 medium onion, chopped
¼ cup chopped green pepper
2 tablespoons butter
1 10¾-ounce can condensed
    cream of mushroom soup
1 cup dairy sour cream
¼ cup milk
¾ cup shredded mozzarella
    cheese (3 ounces)
¾ cup shredded provolone
    cheese (3 ounces)
1 8-ounce package sliced
    bologna *or* salami, cut into
    8 wedges

¾ cup soft rye bread crumbs
    (1 slice)
1 tablespoon butter, melted

Cook noodles according to package directions; drain. Cook onion and green pepper in the 2 tablespoons butter till tender. Remove from heat. Stir in soup, sour cream, and milk. Stir in the cooked noodles, both cheeses, and bologna. Turn into a 2-quart casserole. Cover and refrigerate for 3 to 24 hours.

Before serving: Mix crumbs and 1 tablespoon butter; sprinkle atop casserole. Bake in 350° oven 45 to 50 minutes. Serves 4.

Spicy Sausage Sandwiches

½ pound bulk Italian sausage
¼ cup chopped onion
⅓ cup sliced pitted ripe olives
¼ cup catsup
1 teaspoon dried basil, crushed
½ teaspoon dried oregano,
    crushed
4 French-style rolls (6 inches
    long)
8 slices Muenster *or*
    mozzarella cheese

Cook sausage and onion till meat is browned. Drain off fat. Remove from heat. Stir in olives, catsup, basil, and oregano.

Split rolls lengthwise. Place a cheese slice, cut to fit, on bottom half of roll. Spoon about ⅓ cup meat mixture atop. Place another slice cheese atop meat. Top with roll top. Repeat with remaining rolls. Wrap each in foil. Refrigerate for 2 to 24 hours.

Before serving: Place foil-wrapped sandwiches on baking sheet. Bake in 375° oven about 20 minutes. Makes 4 servings.

● **Freezer Sausage Sandwiches:** Prepare Spicy Sausage Sandwiches as directed above, wrapping in heavy foil. Seal, label, and freeze. Before serving, place foil-wrapped sandwiches on a baking sheet. Bake in a 375° oven for 30 to 35 minutes.

Sausage-Potato Bake

3 medium potatoes, peeled and
    thinly sliced
½ cup chopped onion
½ cup chopped green pepper
1 pound fully cooked smoked
    sausage, cut into ½-inch
    slices
1 3-ounce package cream
    cheese
⅓ cup milk
½ cup dairy sour cream
1 tablespoon all-purpose flour
½ teaspoon dried thyme,
    crushed

Cook potatoes, onion, and green pepper in boiling water till tender; drain. Turn into a 1½-quart casserole. Add sliced sausage; toss lightly. Cut up cream cheese. Cook and stir cream cheese and milk till cream cheese melts. Remove from heat. Stir in sour cream, flour, thyme, and ⅛ teaspoon *pepper.* Pour over potato mixture; stir. Cover and refrigerate for 3 to 24 hours.

Before serving: Bake in 350° oven about 50 minutes. Serves 4.

Poultry

Chicken Kiev

2 whole large chicken breasts, skinned, halved lengthwise, and boned
2 tablespoons chopped green onion
1 tablespoon snipped parsley
6 tablespoons stick butter *or* margarine, well chilled
2 tablespoons all-purpose flour
1 beaten egg
⅓ cup fine dry bread crumbs
2 tablespoons butter *or* margarine

Pound each piece of chicken breast half to ⅛-inch thickness, working from center. Sprinkle one side of chicken with green onion and parsley. Season with salt and pepper.

Cut the 6 tablespoons stick butter or margarine lengthwise into 4 sticks, each about 2 inches long. Place one stick on the seasoned side of each chicken piece. Fold in sides; roll up jelly-roll style; seal ends. Coat rolls with flour; dip in egg, then in crumbs. Cover and refrigerate for 2 to 24 hours.

Before serving: In skillet cook chicken rolls in the 2 tablespoons butter or margarine for 5 minutes or till brown. Transfer to an 8x8x2-inch baking dish. Bake in a 400° oven for 15 to 20 minutes or till done. Makes 4 servings.

Stuffed Chicken Rolls
Turkey and Rice Pie
(see recipe, page 38)

Stuffed Chicken Rolls

Pictured on the cover —

1½ cups chopped mushrooms
½ teaspoon dried thyme, crushed
3 tablespoons butter
1 10-ounce package frozen chopped spinach, cooked and well-drained
3 hard-cooked eggs, chopped
3 whole medium chicken breasts, skinned, halved lengthwise, and boned
6 frozen patty shells, thawed
1 beaten egg
Tomato *or* Wine Sauce
Green Rice (optional)

Cook mushrooms and thyme in butter till tender; mix with spinach and eggs. Pound chicken to flatten slightly. Season. Spoon ½ *cup* of spinach mixture in center; roll up. Roll out each patty shell to accommodate chicken roll (about 8x6 inches). Place chicken roll, seam side down, on pastry. Fold up pastry edges; seal. Place, seam side down, in 15x10x1-inch baking pan. Combine egg and 1 tablespoon *water*. Brush over rolls. Cover and refrigerate for 2 to 24 hours.

Before serving: Bake in 400° oven 50 to 60 minutes. Cover with foil after 40 minutes. Prepare Tomato Sauce or Wine Sauce; spoon over chicken rolls. Sprinkle with snipped parsley or fresh dill and serve atop Green Rice, if desired. Serves 6.

Tomato Sauce: Blend one 7½-ounce can *tomatoes*, cut up, and ⅓ cup *chicken broth* into 1 tablespoon *cornstarch*. Add 1½ teaspoons *sugar*, 1 teaspoon *Worces-*

tershire sauce, and ½ teaspoon dried *thyme*, crushed. Cook and stir till bubbly. Continue 2 minutes more. Stir in ⅓ cup *dry white wine*.

Wine Sauce: Melt 3 tablespoons *butter*. Stir in 3 tablespoons all-purpose *flour*, ½ teaspoon *salt*, and dash *pepper*. Add 1¼ cups *light cream*. Cook and stir till bubbly. Continue 1 minute more. Stir in ¼ cup *dry white wine*. Add ⅓ cup shredded *Swiss cheese*; stir till melted.

Green Rice: Cook ¼ cup sliced *green onion*, ¼ cup finely chopped *green pepper*, 2 tablespoons snipped *parsley*, and 2 tablespoons *butter* till tender. Stir into 3 cups cooked *rice*.

Chicken and Rice Bake

1 14½-ounce can chicken broth
1 10¾-ounce can condensed cream of mushroom soup
1 cup long grain rice
1 4-ounce can sliced mushrooms, drained
1 2-ounce jar sliced pimiento, drained and chopped
½ cup chopped onion
1 tablespoon snipped parsley
½ teaspoon poultry seasoning
1 2½- to 3-pound broiler-fryer chicken, cut up
Paprika

Combine first 8 ingredients. Turn into 13x9x2-inch baking dish. Place chicken atop; season. Cover; refrigerate for 2 to 24 hours.

Before serving: Bake, covered, in 350° oven about 1¼ hours. Stir rice; sprinkle with paprika. Bake, uncovered, 15 minutes more. Skim off fat. Stir rice. Serves 6.

Poultry

Chicken Pajarski

- 3 whole large chicken breasts, skinned and boned
- 6 tablespoons butter *or* margarine, melted
- ¼ teaspoon ground nutmeg
- ½ cup all-purpose flour
- 2 eggs
- 2 tablespoons water
- 2 teaspoons cooking oil
- 2½ to 3 cups soft bread crumbs
- ½ cup butter *or* margarine
  Snipped parsley
  Paprika Sauce

Chill a large mixing bowl. Grind chicken through fine blade of food grinder or finely chop. In chilled bowl combine chicken, the melted butter or margarine, nutmeg, ½ teaspoon *salt,* and ⅛ teaspoon *pepper.* Mix well. Chill in the freezer, but *do not freeze.* In a small bowl combine flour with ½ teaspoon *salt* and dash *pepper.* In another small bowl beat eggs with water and oil. Divide chilled chicken mixture into 12 equal portions. Shape each portion into a ball, then flatten balls to ½-inch thickness. Dip patties, one at a time, in flour mixture, then dip in egg mixture and bread crumbs. Press crumbs into meat with fingers. Cover and refrigerate for 2 to 24 hours. Make Paprika Sauce.

Before serving: In large skillet heat the ½ cup butter. Carefully add patties. Cook over medium-low heat about 20 minutes or till patties are brown and chicken is done, turning once. Arrange on hot platter. Garnish with parsley. Serve with Paprika Sauce. Serves 6.

Paprika Sauce: In saucepan melt ¼ cup *butter or margarine;* add ⅓ cup chopped *onion* and cook till onion is tender but not brown. Stir in 2 tablespoons all-purpose *flour,* 4 teaspoons *paprika,* and 1 teaspoon dried *thyme,* crushed. Add 1 cup *chicken broth* and 1 cup *whipping cream* all at once. Cook and stir till bubbly. Reduce heat; stir in 4 teaspoons *lemon juice,* 2 teaspoons *brandy,* ¼ teaspoon *salt,* and a dash *pepper.* Strain sauce. Cover and chill. Before serving, stir in ½ cup *dairy sour cream;* heat through but *do not boil.*

Soy-Marinated Chicken

- 1 2½- to 3-pound broiler-fryer chicken, cut up
- ¼ cup soy sauce
- 2 teaspoons finely shredded lemon peel
- ¼ cup lemon juice
- 2 tablespoons cooking oil
- 1 clove garlic, minced

Place chicken in a plastic bag; set in a baking dish. For marinade, combine soy sauce, lemon peel, lemon juice, oil, and garlic; pour over chicken. Close bag. Refrigerate for 3 to 24 hours, turning bag occasionally.

Before serving: Drain chicken, reserving marinade. Place chicken pieces, skin side down, on rack of unheated broiler pan. Broil 5 to 6 inches from heat about 20 minutes or till lightly browned. Turn; broil 15 to 20 minutes more. Brush often with marinade. Serves 6.

Honey-Glazed Chicken

- 1 2½- to 3-pound broiler-fryer chicken, cut up
- 2 tablespoons cooking oil
- ½ cup orange juice
- 2 tablespoons soy sauce
- 1 teaspoon grated fresh gingerroot
- 2 tablespoons cold water
- 1 tablespoon cornstarch
- ¼ cup honey
  Hot cooked rice (optional)

In large skillet cook chicken pieces in hot oil about 15 minutes or till brown, turning often. Drain off fat. Stir in orange juice, soy sauce, and gingerroot. Cover and simmer about 30 minutes or till chicken is tender.

Transfer chicken to 12x7½x2-inch baking dish. Skim excess fat from pan juices. For honey glaze, measure pan juices and add water, if necessary, to make ½ cup liquid. Combine cold water and cornstarch; stir into pan juice liquid. Cook and stir till thickened and bubbly. Cook and stir 1 to 2 minutes more. Stir in honey. Spoon honey glaze over chicken. Cover and refrigerate for 3 to 24 hours.

Before serving: Bake, covered, in a 375° oven about 40 minutes or till done. Serve with hot cooked rice, if desired. Makes 6 servings.

Poultry

Coronado Chicken

1 2½- to 3-pound broiler-fryer
  chicken, cut up
2 tablespoons butter
½ cup chopped onion
1 clove garlic, minced
1 8-ounce can tomato sauce
1 cup beer *or* chicken broth
1 teaspoon paprika
1 teaspoon chili powder
1 teaspoon Worcestershire
  sauce
½ cup dairy sour cream
2 tablespoons cornstarch
1 10-ounce package frozen
  peas and carrots
  Hot cooked rice (optional)

In Dutch oven cook chicken in butter about 15 minutes or till brown, turning often; remove chicken and set aside. Add onion and garlic to pan; cook till tender but not brown. Drain off fat. Stir in tomato sauce, beer or chicken broth, paprika, chili powder, Worcestershire sauce, and 1 teaspoon *salt*. Bring to boiling; add chicken. Reduce heat; cover and simmer about 45 minutes or till chicken is tender. Transfer chicken to 12x7½x2-inch baking dish. Skim excess fat from pan juices. Combine sour cream and cornstarch. Stir about *half* of the hot pan juices into the sour cream; return all to pan. Cook and stir till mixture is thickened and bubbly. Cook and stir 1 to 2 minutes longer. Stir in frozen peas and carrots. Pour sauce over chicken. Cover and refrigerate for 3 to 24 hours.

Before serving: Bake, covered, in 375° oven about 60 minutes. Serve with hot cooked rice, if desired. Serves 6.

Chicken with Beer

¼ cup all-purpose flour
1 teaspoon salt
½ teaspoon dried rosemary,
  crushed
⅛ teaspoon pepper
1 2½- to 3-pound broiler-fryer
  chicken, cut up
2 tablespoons cooking oil
½ cup chopped onion *or*
  chopped green pepper
1 10¾-ounce can condensed
  cream of onion soup
¾ cup beer
  Hot cooked noodles
  (optional)

In plastic bag combine flour, salt, rosemary, and pepper. Add chicken pieces, a few at a time; shake to coat.

In skillet cook chicken pieces in hot oil about 15 minutes or till brown, turning often; transfer to 3-quart casserole. In same skillet cook onion or green pepper till tender but not brown. Drain off fat. Stir in soup and beer; pour over chicken. Cover and refrigerate for 3 to 24 hours.

Before serving: Bake, covered, in a 350° oven about 1 hour or till tender. Skim excess fat. Serve over hot cooked noodles, if desired. Makes 6 servings.

● **Microwave directions:** Prepare Chicken with Beer as directed above *except* turn mixture into a 3-quart nonmetal casserole. Refrigerate as directed above. Before serving, cook, covered, in a counter-top microwave oven on high power for 20 to 25 minutes or till chicken is done, rearranging pieces once or twice. Skim excess fat before serving.

Creamy Chicken Mousse

1 3-ounce package lemon-
  flavored gelatin
½ cup boiling water
½ cup cold water
1 tablespoon minced dried
  onion
2 teaspoons lemon juice
  Dash bottled hot pepper
  sauce
¾ cup mayonnaise *or* salad
  dressing
½ cup plain yogurt
2 5½-ounce cans boned
  chicken, drained and
  chopped
2 tablespoons finely chopped
  celery
  Curly endive (optional)
  Cherry tomatoes (optional)

Dissolve lemon gelatin in boiling water. Stir in cold water, dried onion, lemon juice, and hot pepper sauce. Beat in mayonnaise or salad dressing and yogurt. Pour into shallow pan. Freeze about 15 minutes or till edges are firm and center is soft. Meanwhile, in bowl combine chicken and celery; set aside. Spoon gelatin mixture into mixer bowl. Beat with electric mixer about 3 minutes till fluffy. Fold in chicken mixture. Pour into a 4- to 5-cup mold. Refrigerate for 6 to 24 hours.

Before serving: Unmold onto serving plate. If desired, garnish with curly endive and cherry tomatoes. Makes 4 servings.

Poultry

Turkey Stuffing Bake

1 cup herb-seasoned stuffing
mix
⅓ cup water
2 tablespoons butter *or*
margarine
1 cup finely chopped peeled
apple
½ cup chopped celery
¼ cup chopped onion
2 tablespoons snipped parsley
½ teaspoon salt
¼ teaspoon poultry seasoning
⅛ teaspoon pepper
2 cups chopped cooked turkey

Prepare stuffing mix according to package directions *except* use the ⅓ cup water and 2 tablespoons butter or margarine. Add apple, celery, onion, parsley, salt, poultry seasoning, and pepper; toss to mix. Add turkey; toss well. Turn mixture into a 1½-quart casserole. Cover and refrigerate for 3 to 24 hours.

Before serving: Bake, covered, in a 375° oven about 30 minutes. Uncover and bake 5 minutes longer or till heated through. Makes 4 servings.

● **Microwave directions:** Prepare Turkey Stuffing Bake as directed above *except* turn into a nonmetal 1½-quart casserole. Refrigerate as directed above.

Before serving, cook, covered, in a counter-top microwave oven on high power about 15 minutes or till heated through, stirring once.

Turkey and Rice Pie

Pictured on page 34 —

Pastry for Double Crust Pie
(see recipe, page 40)
2 5-ounce cans boned turkey,
drained
1 cup cooked rice
½ cup frozen peas
½ cup shredded cheddar
cheese (2 ounces)
2 hard-cooked eggs, chopped
¼ teaspoon salt
½ cup chopped onion
2 tablespoons butter *or*
margarine
1 3-ounce package cream
cheese, cut up
⅓ cup milk

Prepare Pastry. On floured surface roll 1 ball of dough to a 12-inch circle. Transfer to a 9-inch pie plate; trim pastry to ½-inch beyond edge of pie plate; set aside.

In bowl combine turkey, rice, peas, cheddar cheese, eggs, and salt; set aside. In saucepan cook onion in butter or margarine till tender. Stir in cream cheese and milk. Cook and stir till cheese melts; stir into rice mixture. Turn into pastry shell.

Roll out remaining dough. Cut into ½-inch strips; weave atop filling, twisting, if desired. Press ends of strips into rim of crust; fold bottom pastry over strips. Seal and flute. (Or, seal and twist additional strips around edge.) Cover and refrigerate 3 to 24 hours.

Before serving: Brush top with additional milk. Bake in 375° oven 70 to 75 minutes. If necessary, cover pastry edge with foil to prevent overbrowning. Serves 6.

Orange-Stuffed Cornish Hens

3 1- to 1½-pound Cornish
game hens, thawed
Cooking oil
1 11-ounce can mandarin
orange sections
¼ teaspoon salt
⅛ teaspoon ground sage
1½ cups toasted whole wheat
bread cubes (3 slices)
¼ cup finely chopped celery
1 tablespoon butter *or*
margarine, melted
2 tablespoons butter *or*
margarine, melted

Halve hens lengthwise. Season cavities of hens with salt. Brush skin with cooking oil; place in bowl. Cover and refrigerate for 3 to 24 hours.

Drain orange sections, reserving ¼ cup syrup. Halve orange sections. In bowl combine orange sections, salt, and sage. Add bread cubes, celery, and the 1 tablespoon melted butter or margarine. Toss lightly to mix. Using a ⅓ cup measure, shape stuffing into 6 mounds. Place in bottom of 13x9x2-inch baking dish. Cover and refrigerate for 2 to 24 hours.

Before serving: Place hens, cut side down, over stuffing mounds in baking dish. Roast, covered, in a 375° oven for 40 minutes. Combine reserved mandarin orange syrup and the 2 tablespoons melted butter or margarine. Uncover birds; baste with orange-butter mixture. Roast, uncovered, for 20 to 25 minutes more or till drumsticks can be twisted easily, basting once or twice with orange-butter mixture. Makes 6 servings.

Fish

Hawaiian Fish Kebabs

1 pound fresh *or* frozen fish
   fillets
3 tablespoons cooking oil
3 tablespoons soy sauce
1 tablespoon light corn syrup
1 clove garlic, minced
½ teaspoon dry mustard
½ teaspoon ground ginger
1 large green *or* red sweet
   pepper
6 bacon slices, cut into 1-inch
   pieces
1 15½-ounce can pineapple
   chunks, drained
   Hot cooked rice (optional)

Thaw fish, if frozen. Cut into 1-inch pieces. For marinade, in bowl combine cooking oil, soy sauce, corn syrup, minced garlic, dry mustard, and ginger. Place fish pieces in marinade. Cover and refrigerate for 3 to 24 hours.

Cut green or red sweet pepper into 1-inch squares; cover and refrigerate. In skillet partially cook bacon; remove from skillet, cover and refrigerate.

Before serving: Drain fish, reserving marinade. On 4 skewers alternate fish, green or red sweet pepper, bacon, and pineapple chunks. Place on rack of unheated broiler pan. Broil 4 inches from heat for 10 to 12 minutes, turning and basting frequently with marinade. Serve with hot cooked rice, if desired. Makes 4 servings.

Stuffed Swiss Fillets

2 pounds fresh *or* frozen fish
   fillets (8 fillets)
⅓ cup long grain rice
2 tablespoons chopped onion
5 tablespoons butter *or*
   margarine
1½ teaspoons instant chicken
   bouillon granules
1 3-ounce can chopped
   mushrooms, drained
3 tablespoons all-purpose flour
1½ cups milk
½ cup dry white wine
1 cup shredded process Swiss
   cheese
   Paprika

Thaw fish, if frozen. Meanwhile, in saucepan cook uncooked rice and onion in *2 tablespoons* of the butter for 5 to 8 minutes or till rice is brown, stirring often. Stir in bouillon granules and 1 cup *water*. Bring to boiling; reduce heat. Cover and cook for 20 to 25 minutes or till rice is fluffy. Stir in mushrooms.

Place about ¼ *cup* of the rice mixture atop *each* fillet; wrap fillet around mixture. Place, seam side down, in a 10x6x2-inch baking dish. Cover and refrigerate for 2 to 24 hours.

Before serving: In saucepan melt the remaining butter or margarine; stir in flour, ¼ teaspoon *salt,* and dash *pepper.* Add milk all at once. Cook and stir till thickened and bubbly. Cook and stir 1 to 2 minutes more. Stir in wine. Pour over fillets. Bake, uncovered, in 400° oven about 45 minutes. Sprinkle with cheese and paprika. Continue baking 5 to 10 minutes more or till fish flakes easily when tested with fork. Makes 8 servings.

Fish Fillets with Almonds

Thaw frozen fish in the refrigerator in its original packaging, if desired. One pound takes about 24 hours to thaw—

1 pound fresh *or* frozen fish
   fillets
½ cup water
¼ cup dry sherry
2 teaspoons soy sauce
2 teaspoons instant chicken
   bouillon granules
¼ teaspoon ground ginger
½ cup thinly sliced carrot
½ cup thinly sliced celery
⅓ cup sliced almonds

Let frozen fish stand at room temperature 20 minutes. Cut fish fillets crosswise into 4 serving-size portions. Place fish portions in a skillet.

In a bowl combine water, dry sherry, soy sauce, chicken bouillon granules, and ginger. Pour over fish in skillet. Add carrot and celery. Bring to boiling; reduce heat. Cover and simmer for 5 minutes or till fish flakes easily when tested with a fork. Remove from heat. Carefully transfer fillets to a 12x7½x2-inch baking dish; pour vegetables and liquid over fish. Cover and refrigerate for 3 to 24 hours.

Before serving: Sprinkle fish fillets with almonds. Bake, uncovered, in 375° oven for 15 to 20 minutes or till heated through. Makes 4 servings.

Fish

Cool Coulibiac

Pastry for Double Crust Pie
1 cup shredded carrot
½ cup finely chopped onion
½ cup finely chopped celery
3 tablespoons cooking oil
1 cup thinly sliced fresh
    mushrooms
⅓ cup dairy sour cream
2 tablespoons lemon juice
1½ teaspoons finely snipped
    fresh dill *or* ½ teaspoon
    dried dillweed
1 15½-ounce can salmon,
    drained, lightly flaked, skin
    and bones removed
1 beaten egg
Dairy sour cream

Prepare Pastry; set aside. For filling, cook carrot, onion, and celery in hot oil, covered, till vegetables are tender. Remove from heat. Stir in mushrooms, the ⅓ cup sour cream, lemon juice, dill or dillweed, ½ teaspoon *salt,* and ¼ teaspoon *pepper.* Gently stir in salmon.

On floured surface roll *half* of the pastry to a 15x7-inch rectangle. Cut crosswise into thirds, forming three 7x5-inch pieces. (Trim into shell shapes, if desired.) Place pastries on ungreased baking sheet. Spoon about ½ cup of the filling on half of *each* pastry; moisten edges. Fold other half of each pastry over filling. Seal with tines of fork. Repeat with remaining pastry and filling. Combine egg and 1 tablespoon *water;* brush tops of pastry. Slit tops. Bake in 400° oven for 20 to 25 minutes. Cover and refrigerate for 3 to 24 hours.

Before serving: Dollop with sour cream. Serves 6.

Pastry for Double Crust Pie: In mixing bowl combine 2 cups all-purpose *flour* and 1 teaspoon *salt.* Cut in ⅔ cup *shortening or lard* till mixture resembles small peas. Sprinkle 1 tablespoon *cold water* over part of mixture; gently toss with fork; then push to side of bowl. Repeat, using 5 to 6 more tablespoons cold *water,* till all is moistened. Form dough into 2 balls.

Citrus Salmon Steaks

1½ pounds fresh *or* frozen
    salmon steaks (1 inch
    thick)
2 tablespoons frozen grapefruit
    juice concentrate, thawed
1 tablespoon thinly sliced green
    onion
1 tablespoon cooking oil
1 tablespoon lemon juice
¼ teaspoon dried rosemary,
    crushed

Thaw steaks, if frozen. Place steaks in plastic bag; set in shallow pan. For marinade, combine juice concentrate, green onion, cooking oil, lemon juice, rosemary, ½ cup *water,* and ¼ teaspoon *salt;* pour over steaks in bag. Close bag. Refrigerate for 3 to 24 hours, turning bag occasionally.

Before serving: Drain off marinade; set aside. Place fish on rack of unheated broiler pan. Broil 3 to 4 inches from heat about 5 minutes. Brush with marinade; turn and brush again. Broil salmon steaks about 5 minutes more or till done. Makes 4 servings.

Haddock Newburg

1 pound fresh *or* frozen
    haddock fillets
¼ cup butter *or* margarine
2 tablespoons all-purpose flour
1⅔ cups milk
3 beaten egg yolks
⅓ cup dry white wine
1 2-ounce jar sliced pimiento,
    drained and chopped
1 tablespoon lemon juice
4 frozen patty shells
Alfalfa sprouts (optional)

Thaw fish, if frozen. In skillet cover fish with salted water. Bring to boiling; reduce heat. Cover and simmer 5 to 10 minutes or till fish flakes easily when tested with fork. Drain fish; break into large chunks. Set aside.

Melt butter; stir in flour. Add milk all at once. Cook and stir till thickened and bubbly. Stir about *half* of the hot mixture into yolks; return all to hot mixture. Cook and stir till thickened. Gently stir in fish, wine, pimiento, lemon juice, ½ teaspoon *salt,* and dash *pepper.* Cover and refrigerate for 3 to 24 hours.

Before serving: Bake patty shells according to package directions. Meanwhile, cook fish mixture about 10 minutes or till heated through, stirring occasionally. Serve in patty shells atop alfalfa sprouts, if desired. Serves 4.

Cool Coulibiac
Haddock Newburg
Chilled Tarragon Scallop Salad
(see recipe, page 42)

Fish and Seafood

Potato Tuna Patties

2 beaten eggs
2 tablespoons finely chopped onion
2 tablespoons finely chopped green pepper
2 tablespoons all-purpose flour
¼ teaspoon lemon pepper
1 12½-ounce can tuna, drained and flaked
2 cups shredded potatoes
  Shortening or cooking oil for frying
1 cup sour cream dip with French onion

In mixing bowl stir together beaten eggs, chopped onion, chopped green pepper, all-purpose flour, and lemon pepper. Stir in flaked tuna and uncooked shredded potatoes. In skillet heat about ⅛-inch shortening or oil. For each patty, drop ⅓ *cup* of the mixture into skillet; flatten slightly with a spatula. Cook for 6 to 8 minutes or till lightly browned, turning once. Drain on paper toweling. Cover and refrigerate for 2 to 24 hours.

Before serving: Place chilled patties on baking sheet. Bake in 350° oven about 25 minutes or till heated through. Heat sour cream dip with French onion on low heat, stirring constantly, just till warm. Serve heated dip with patties. Makes 6 servings.

Tuna and Pepper Salad

2 medium green peppers
1 cup shredded carrot
1 cup sliced celery
1 6½-ounce can tuna, drained and flaked
2 tablespoons chopped onion
½ cup mayonnaise or salad dressing
1 tablespoon vinegar
1 tablespoon prepared mustard
2 teaspoons sugar
¼ teaspoon salt
  Lettuce leaves

Cut green peppers into rings. Cover and refrigerate. In mixing bowl combine shredded carrot, sliced celery, tuna, and onion.

Stir together mayonnaise or salad dressing, vinegar, mustard, sugar, and salt. Pour over tuna mixture and toss lightly. Cover and refrigerate for 3 to 24 hours.

Before serving: Line 4 salad plates with lettuce; arrange pepper rings atop. Spoon tuna mixture over peppers. Makes 4 servings.

Cooling tip

Do not let foods that need refrigerating stand at room temperature to cool. Since large volumes of hot food can raise the temperature inside the refrigerator or freezer, cool food quickly by placing in a shallow container and setting container in a pan of ice water.

Chilled Tarragon Scallop Salad

Pictured on page 41 —

¾ pound fresh or frozen scallops
1 cup water
½ teaspoon salt
1 medium tomato, peeled and chopped
½ cup bias-sliced celery
¼ cup sliced green onion
¼ cup white wine vinegar
2 tablespoons olive oil or salad oil
1 teaspoon honey
¾ teaspoon dried tarragon, crushed
½ teaspoon salt
  Dash pepper
1 6-ounce package frozen pea pods
  Lettuce leaves
4 hard-cooked eggs, sliced

Thaw scallops, if frozen. Cut any large scallops in half. In saucepan bring water and salt to boiling; add scallops and return to boiling. Simmer 1 minute; drain and cool.

In bowl combine scallops, tomato, celery, and green onion. In screw-top jar combine white wine vinegar, olive oil or salad oil, honey, tarragon, salt, and pepper. Cover and shake well. Pour over scallop mixture; toss to coat. Cover and refrigerate for 3 to 24 hours.

Before serving: Run hot water over frozen pea pods till thawed. Drain scallop mixture and spoon onto 4 lettuce-lined plates. Arrange pea pods around mixture. Garnish with egg slices. Makes 4 servings.

Seafood

Cavatelli Shrimp Salad

Cavatelli are elongated, shell-shaped pasta. Substitute seashell or elbow macaroni if you do not have cavatelli on hand—

- 6 cups water
- 1 tablespoon salt
- 1 pound fresh *or* frozen shelled shrimp
- 1½ cups cavatelli, cooked and drained
- 4 ounces colby cheese, cubed (1 cup)
- ½ cup chopped celery
- ¼ cup chopped green pepper
- 2 tablespoons chopped onion
- ½ cup mayonnaise *or* salad dressing
- ½ cup dairy sour cream
- 3 tablespoons vinegar
- 2 tablespoons milk
- ½ teaspoon salt
  Dash bottled hot pepper sauce
  Lettuce leaves
  Green pepper rings (optional)

In large saucepan combine water and salt. Bring to boiling. Add fresh or frozen shrimp. Simmer 1 to 3 minutes or till shrimp turn pink. Drain and cool.

In bowl combine shrimp, cavatelli, cheese, celery, green pepper, and onion. Combine mayonnaise or salad dressing, sour cream, vinegar, milk, salt, and hot pepper sauce. Pour mayonnaise mixture over shrimp mixture; toss well. Cover and refrigerate for 3 to 24 hours.

Before serving: Toss well. Spoon into lettuce-lined bowl. Top with green pepper rings, if desired. Makes 6 servings.

Manhatten Clam Chowder

- 1 pint shucked clams *or* two 6½-ounce cans minced clams
- 3 slices bacon, cut up
- 1 cup finely chopped celery
- 1 cup chopped onion
- 1 16-ounce can tomatoes
- 2 medium potatoes, peeled and chopped
- ½ cup finely chopped carrots
- ½ teaspoon dried thyme, crushed

Drain clams, reserving liquid. Chop shucked clams. Add enough water to reserved liquid to measure 3 cups. Partially cook bacon; add celery and onion. Cook and stir till vegetables are tender. Cut up tomatoes. Stir in clam juice mixture, *undrained* tomatoes, potatoes, carrots, thyme, 1 teaspoon *salt* and ⅛ teaspoon *pepper*. Bring to boiling; reduce heat. Cover; simmer 30 to 35 minutes. Mash vegetables slightly. Add clams. Turn into covered container. Refrigerate 3 to 24 hours.

Before serving: Heat chowder through. Makes 6 to 8 servings.

Buying Frozen Fish and Seafood

When buying frozen fish or seafood, beware of signs of thawing and refreezing, misshapen or torn packages, and containers that have frost or blood visible on the outside or inside. White spots on the contents indicate freezer burn.

Cheesy Crab Strata

To prevent overcooking, test for doneness by inserting a knife 1 to 2 inches off center. The strata will continue to cook after removal from the oven—

- 6 slices white bread
  Prepared mustard
- 1 7-ounce can crab meat, drained, flaked, and cartilage removed
- ¼ cup thinly sliced celery
- 1 tablespoon sliced green onion
- 6 slices American cheese (4 ounces)
- 5 beaten eggs
- 2½ cups milk
  Paprika

Lightly spread one side of *each* bread slice with mustard. Cut slices into thirds. Arrange *half* of the bread, mustard side up, in a greased 8x8x2-inch baking dish. Combine crab, celery, and green onion; sprinkle over bread in baking dish. Top with cheese, then remaining bread, mustard side down. In bowl stir together eggs and milk. Pour egg mixture over bread; sprinkle with paprika. Cover and refrigerate for 3 to 24 hours.

Before serving: Bake strata, uncovered, in 325° oven for 65 to 70 minutes or till knife inserted off center comes out clean. Let stand 5 minutes. Makes 6 servings.

Eggs and Cheese

Cheese Manicotti

Pictured on pages 20 and 21 and on the cover —

¼ cup chopped onion
1 clove garlic, minced
2 tablespoons cooking oil
1 16-ounce can tomatoes, cut up
1 8-ounce can tomato sauce
⅓ cup water
1 teaspoon sugar
1 teaspoon dried oregano, crushed
¼ teaspoon dried thyme, crushed
¼ teaspoon salt
1 small bay leaf
8 manicotti shells
2 beaten eggs
1½ cups ricotta cheese *or* cream-style cottage cheese
2 cups shredded mozzarella cheese (8 ounces)
½ cup grated Parmesan cheese
¼ cup snipped parsley
½ teaspoon dried oregano, crushed
¼ teaspoon salt

In a 2-quart saucepan cook onion and garlic in oil till tender but not brown. Add *undrained* tomatoes, tomato sauce, water, sugar, the 1 teaspoon oregano, the thyme, ¼ teaspoon salt, and the bay leaf. Bring to boiling; simmer, uncovered, 45 minutes. Remove bay leaf; discard.

Meanwhile, cook manicotti shells in boiling salted water just till tender; drain. Rinse shells with cold water. Combine eggs, ricotta or cottage cheese, *half* of the mozzarella cheese, Parmesan, parsley, the

½ teaspoon oregano, ¼ teaspoon salt, and dash *pepper*. Spoon cheese mixture into manicotti shells.

Pour *half* of the tomato mixture into a 10x6x2-inch baking dish. Arrange stuffed manicotti shells in baking dish. Pour remaining sauce over shells. Sprinkle remaining mozzarella cheese atop. Cover; refrigerate for 3 to 24 hours.

Before serving: Bake manicotti, covered, in a 350° oven for 35 to 40 minutes or till hot and bubbly. Makes 6 servings.

Cheese and Egg Salad Sandwiches

¼ cup mayonnaise *or* salad dressing
2 tablespoons finely chopped green onion
1 tablespoon sweet pickle relish
¼ teaspoon dried dillweed
Dash salt
Dash pepper
4 hard-cooked eggs, coarsely chopped
4 lettuce leaves
8 slices bread *or* toast
4 slices cheddar cheese (4 ounces)

In bowl combine mayonnaise or salad dressing, chopped green onion, sweet pickle relish, dillweed, salt, and pepper. Add eggs; toss to mix. Cover and refrigerate 3 to 24 hours.

Before serving: Place lettuce leaves on *half* of bread or toast slices. Spoon egg mixture atop. Top with slice of cheese, then remaining bread. Makes 4 servings.

Vegetable and Noodle Casserole

1 stalk celery, chopped
1 medium onion, chopped
1 small green pepper, chopped
2 tablespoons butter *or* margarine
½ cup milk
1 tablespoon cornstarch
¾ teaspoon salt
⅛ teaspoon pepper
2 cups noodles, cooked and drained
2 cups shredded Monterey Jack cheese (8 ounces)
1 cup fresh *or* frozen cut broccoli, cooked and drained
¼ cup fine dry bread crumbs
¼ cup shredded Monterey Jack cheese (1 ounce)
1 tablespoon toasted wheat germ
1 tablespoon butter, melted

Cook celery, onion, and green pepper in the 2 tablespoons butter till tender but not brown. Combine milk and cornstarch. Add to vegetables along with salt and pepper. Cook and stir till thickened and bubbly. Cook and stir 1 to 2 minutes more. Remove from heat. Combine noodles, the 2 cups cheese, broccoli, and the celery mixture. Turn into an ungreased 1½-quart casserole. Cover and refrigerate for 3 to 24 hours.

Before serving: Bake, covered, in a 350° oven for 35 minutes. Combine bread crumbs, ¼ cup cheese, wheat germ, and the 1 tablespoon melted butter. Sprinkle around edge of casserole. Bake, uncovered, 15 minutes more or till heated through. Makes 4 servings.

Eggs and Cheese

Creamy Mexicali Macaroni

- 1 cup elbow macaroni
- 3 eggs
- 2 tablespoons all-purpose flour
- ½ teaspoon salt
- ⅛ teaspoon pepper
- 2 cups shredded Monterey Jack cheese (8 ounces)
- 1 cup milk
- 1 4-ounce can green chili peppers, rinsed, seeded, and chopped
- ¼ cup chopped onion
- ¼ cup chopped celery
- 1 cup taco chips
- 2 tablespoons grated Parmesan cheese

Cook macaroni in large amount of boiling salted water for 7 to 8 minutes or till tender. Drain; set aside. In a mixing bowl beat together eggs, flour, salt, and pepper. Stir in the shredded Monterey Jack cheese, the milk, chopped green chili peppers, chopped onion, chopped celery, and the cooked macaroni. Turn macaroni mixture into an ungreased 1½-quart casserole. Cover and refrigerate for 3 to 24 hours.

Before serving: Crush the taco chips. In a small mixing bowl toss together the crushed chips and Parmesan cheese. Sprinkle chip-cheese mixture over frozen casserole. Bake in a 350° oven for 55 to 60 minutes or till heated through. Makes 4 servings.

Mock Meatballs

- 5 eggs
- 1 cup shredded cheddar cheese
- ½ cup cream-style cottage cheese
- ½ cup finely chopped onion
- 1 teaspoon dried basil, crushed
- ½ teaspoon ground sage
- 2 cups herb-seasoned stuffing mix, crushed
- 1 cup finely chopped walnuts
- 1 8-ounce can tomato sauce
- 1 teaspoon sugar

In mixing bowl beat together eggs, cheddar and cottage cheeses, onion, basil, sage, and ½ teaspoon *salt*. Stir in stuffing mix and nuts; mix well. Shape into 24 "meatballs." Place balls in 12x7½x2-inch baking dish. Cover and refrigerate for 3 to 24 hours.

Before serving: Combine tomato sauce, sugar, and 1 cup *water*; pour *half* over meatballs. Bake, uncovered, in a 350° oven for 50 to 55 minutes. Heat remaining sauce; pass. Makes 6 servings.

Garden Quiche

- ¾ cup all-purpose flour
- ½ cup whole wheat flour
- ⅓ cup shortening
- 4 to 5 tablespoons cold water
- ¾ cup sliced fresh mushrooms
- ¼ cup chopped onion
- ¼ cup chopped green pepper
- 1 clove garlic, minced
- 3 beaten eggs
- 1½ cups light cream *or* milk
- 1 tablespoon all-purpose flour
- 1½ cups shredded Swiss cheese

For pastry, in bowl stir together the ¾ cup all-purpose flour, the whole wheat flour, and ½ teaspoon *salt*. Cut in shortening till pieces resemble small peas. Sprinkle *1 tablespoon* of the cold water over part of the flour mixture; gently toss with a fork. Push to side of bowl; repeat till all is moistened. Form dough into a ball.

On a lightly floured surface roll out dough to about ⅛-inch thickness. Line a 9-inch pie plate or quiche dish with pastry. Trim pastry to ½ inch beyond edge of pie plate. Flute edge of pastry high; *do not prick*. Cover and refrigerate for 3 to 24 hours.

In a saucepan cook mushrooms, onion, green pepper, and garlic in ¼ cup *water* till onion is tender; drain. Cool.

In a mixing bowl beat together eggs, light cream or milk, the 1 tablespoon all-purpose flour, ¼ teaspoon *salt,* and dash *pepper*. Stir in mushroom mixture. Cover and refrigerate for 3 to 24 hours.

Before serving: Line pastry with a double thickness of heavy-duty foil. Bake in a 450° oven for 5 minutes. Carefully remove foil. Bake 5 minutes more or just till golden. Reduce oven temperature to 325°. Sprinkle cheese over hot crust. Pour egg-mushroom mixture over cheese. Bake in 325° oven for 45 to 50 minutes or till almost set in center. If necessary, cover edge of crust with foil to prevent over-browning. Let stand 10 minutes before serving. Makes 6 servings.

Meats

Herbed Steak Supreme

- 2 pounds beef round steak
- 3 tablespoons cooking oil
- 4 medium carrots, thinly sliced (2 cups)
- 2 cups celery cut into 1-inch pieces
- 1 10½-ounce can condensed beef broth
- 1 6-ounce can sliced mushrooms, drained
- 1 medium onion, chopped (½ cup)
- 1 clove garlic, minced
- ¼ cup red wine vinegar
- 2 tablespoons brown sugar
- 1 teaspoon dried basil, crushed
- 1 teaspoon finely shredded lemon peel
- ½ teaspoon paprika
- ⅛ teaspoon pepper
- ¼ cup all-purpose flour
- 1 cup dairy sour cream
  Hot cooked green or regular noodles

Partially freeze meat; cut into bite-size thin strips. In 12-inch skillet quickly brown *half* of the beef at a time in hot cooking oil. Drain off excess fat. Return all meat to skillet. Add carrots, celery, beef broth, mushrooms, onion, garlic, wine vinegar, brown sugar, basil, lemon peel, paprika, and pepper. Bring to boiling. Simmer, covered, about 25 minutes or just till meat and vegetables are tender. Cool slightly. Divide mixture between two 4-cup freezer containers. Cover, seal, label, and freeze.

Before serving: Place one portion frozen meat mixture in a 3-quart saucepan. Add ½ cup *water* for *each* portion. Cook, covered, till heated through. For each portion, blend 2 *tablespoons* flour into ½ *cup* sour cream; stir in some of the hot liquid; add to meat mixture. Cook and stir till thickened and bubbly. Cook and stir 1 to 2 minutes more. Serve over hot cooked noodles. Makes 2 portions, 4 servings each.

Stuffed Meat Rolls

- 2 pounds beef round steak
- 1 teaspoon dried basil, crushed
- ⅛ teaspoon pepper
- 4 ounces thinly sliced prosciutto *or* fully cooked ham, cut into strips
- 4 ounces sliced provolone cheese, cut into strips
- 2 hard-cooked eggs, chopped
- ¼ cup grated Parmesan cheese (1 ounce)
- ½ cup chopped onion
- ¼ cup chopped green pepper
- 1 tablespoon butter *or* margarine
- 1 tablespoon cooking oil
- 1 cup beef broth
- ¼ cup Marsala wine *or* dry sherry
- 2 tablespoons brandy
- ¼ cup cold water
- 2 tablespoons cornstarch
  Hot cooked spaghetti, noodles, *or* rice

Cut round steak into 6 rectangular pieces; pound each piece flat with a meat mallet to about ¼-inch thickness. Combine basil and pepper; sprinkle over meat. Layer a *sixth* of the prosciutto or ham and provolone over each piece of meat. Sprinkle with chopped egg and grated Parmesan. Roll up jelly-roll style from short side and tie with a piece of string.

In large skillet cook onion and green pepper in butter or margarine and cooking oil till tender. Add meat rolls; brown on all sides. Add beef broth and wine or dry sherry. Cover and simmer for 30 minutes. Transfer to a 12x7½x2-inch baking dish. Cover with moisture-vapor-proof wrap. Seal, label, and freeze.

Before serving: Bake, covered, in a 400° oven about 50 minutes or till heated through. Add brandy; bake 10 minutes more. Remove meat rolls to platter and remove strings; keep warm.

Pour broth from baking dish into saucepan. Boil till reduced to 1⅓ cups. Combine cold water and cornstarch; stir into hot broth. Cook and stir till thickened and bubbly. Cook and stir 1 to 2 minutes more. Season to taste with salt and pepper. Serve sauce with meat rolls over the hot cooked spaghetti, noodles, or rice. Makes 6 servings.

Herbed Steak Supreme
Individual Freezer Pizzas
(see recipe, page 48)

Meats

Italian Beef Stew

- 2 pounds beef stew meat, cut into 1-inch cubes
- 2 tablespoons cooking oil
- 1 large onion, chopped
- 1 clove garlic, minced
- 1 16-ounce can tomatoes, cut up
- 1 6-ounce can tomato paste
- ¾ cup dry red wine
- 1½ teaspoons instant beef bouillon granules
- 1 teaspoon dried parsley flakes
- ½ teaspoon dried oregano, crushed
- ½ teaspoon dried basil, crushed
- 3 carrots, sliced (1½ cups)
- 2 stalks celery, sliced
  Grated Parmesan cheese

In Dutch oven brown *half* the meat in hot oil; remove from pan. Brown the remaining meat with the onion and garlic. Drain off fat. Return all meat to pan.

Stir in *undrained* tomatoes, the tomato paste, wine, bouillon granules, parsley, oregano, and basil. Bring to boiling. Cover; simmer 1 to 1¼ hours or till meat is just tender. Add carrots and celery. Cover; simmer 20 minutes more. Cool slightly. Ladle stew into two 4-cup freezer containers. Cover, seal, label, and freeze.

Before serving: Place container in warm water to loosen stew. Remove; place stew in a 1½-quart saucepan. Add ½ cup *water* to each. Heat, covered, over medium-low heat 35 minutes or till thawed, breaking apart with a fork once. Bring to boiling. Serve topped with Parmesan. Makes two 4-cup containers, 4 servings each.

Individual Freezer Pizzas

Pictured on page 47 —

- 1¾ to 2¼ cups all-purpose flour
- ¾ cup whole wheat flour
- 1 package active dry yeast
- 1 cup warm water (115° to 120°)
- 2 tablespoons cooking oil
- 1 pound ground beef *or* pork
- ½ cup chopped onion
- 2 teaspoons dried basil, crushed
- 1 teaspoon dried oregano, crushed
- ½ teaspoon fennel seed, crushed
- 1 15-ounce can tomato sauce
- 2 cups shredded mozzarella cheese (8 ounces)

In mixer bowl combine ¾ *cup* of all-purpose flour, the whole wheat flour, yeast, and 1 teaspoon *salt*. Stir in water and oil. Beat with electric mixer ½ minute. Beat 3 minutes at high speed. Stir in as much of the remaining all-purpose flour as you can mix in with a spoon. Turn out onto lightly floured surface. Knead in enough remaining flour to make a moderately stiff dough that is smooth and elastic (6 to 8 minutes total). Cover; let rest 10 minutes. Divide dough into 6 portions. Roll each into a 6-inch circle. Transfer to greased baking sheets. Build up edges slightly; snip at 1-inch intervals.

Bake in 425° oven 15 minutes or till lightly browned. Remove; cool. Meanwhile, cook meat and onion till meat is browned. Drain off fat. Remove from heat; stir in herbs and ½ teaspoon *salt*. Divide tomato sauce among pizza crusts; spread evenly. Top with meat mixture. Sprinkle cheese atop. Wrap each in moisture-vaporproof wrap. Seal, label, and freeze.

Before serving: Place unwrapped frozen pizza on baking sheet. Bake in 425° oven about 20 minutes or till bubbly. Makes six 5-inch pizzas.

Barley Meat Loaves

- 1 beaten egg
- ¼ cup hot-style catsup
- 1 tablespoon milk
- ¾ cup cooked barley (¼ cup uncooked)
- 2 tablespoons fine dry seasoned bread crumbs
- 2 tablespoons finely chopped onion
- 2 tablespoons chopped green pepper
- 1 teaspoon dried oregano, crushed
- ¾ teaspoon salt
- 1 pound ground beef
  Hot-style catsup

Combine egg, ¼ cup catsup, and milk. Stir in barley, bread crumbs, onion, green pepper, oregano, and salt. Add beef; mix well. Shape mixture into four 4x2-inch loaves. Place in baking pan; freeze till firm. Wrap loaves in moisture-vaporproof wrap. Seal, label, and freeze.

Before serving: Unwrap desired number of loaves. Place in shallow baking pan. Bake, covered, in 400° oven about 50 minutes. Drain off fat; spoon additional catsup over each. Bake, uncovered, 15 minutes more. Makes 4 loaves, 1 serving each.

Meats

Meatballs Bourguignonne

1 beaten egg
¼ cup milk
¾ cup soft whole wheat bread crumbs (1 slice)
2 tablespoons chopped onion
¼ teaspoon salt
Dash pepper
1 pound ground beef
1 10¾-ounce can condensed cream of mushroom soup
½ cup burgundy
2 tablespoons snipped parsley
¼ teaspoon dried thyme, crushed
¼ cup water
Hot cooked noodles

In mixing bowl stir together the egg and milk. Stir in bread crumbs, onion, salt, and pepper. Add ground beef; mix well. With wet hands, shape mixture into 1-inch meatballs. Place meatballs in a 15x10x1-inch baking pan. Bake, uncovered, in a 375° oven for 25 to 30 minutes or till done. Drain off fat.

Arrange meatballs on baking sheet; freeze till firm. Transfer to a 6-cup freezer container. Stir together mushroom soup, burgundy, parsley, and thyme; pour over meatballs. Cover, seal, label and freeze.

Before serving: Transfer frozen meatball mixture to a 3-quart saucepan. Add water. Cover and heat for 20 to 25 minutes or till heated through, gently stirring once or twice. Serve with noodles. Makes 4 to 6 servings.

Hearty Lamb Stew

Taste the hint of sweetness from the apple cider —

1 pound boneless lamb, cut into 1-inch cubes
1½ cups water
½ cup chopped onion
½ cup apple cider *or* apple juice
1 tablespoon instant beef bouillon granules
¼ teaspoon dried savory, crushed
¼ teaspoon dried basil, crushed
⅛ teaspoon pepper
4 carrots, thinly sliced
2 stalks celery, cut into 1-inch pieces
1 9-ounce package frozen cut green beans

In a 3-quart saucepan combine cubed lamb, water, chopped onion, apple cider or apple juice, instant beef bouillon granules, savory, basil, and pepper. Bring meat mixture to boiling. Reduce heat; cover and simmer for 1 hour.

Stir in the sliced carrots and cut-up celery. Cover and cook about 10 minutes more or till vegetables are just tender. Stir in frozen green beans. Cool quickly. Pour meat-vegetable mixture into a 6-cup freezer container. Cover, seal, label, and freeze.

Before serving: In a 3-quart covered saucepan cook frozen stew about 30 minutes or till heated through, stirring occasionally. Makes 4 servings.

Freezer Stuffed Peppers

Pictured on pages 20 and 21 —

6 large green peppers
1 pound ground pork
½ cup chopped onion
1 16-ounce can tomatoes, cut up
½ cup long grain rice
½ cup water
¼ cup finely chopped celery
½ teaspoon instant chicken bouillon granules
¼ teaspoon dried basil, crushed
¼ teaspoon dried thyme, crushed
1 cup shredded cheddar cheese (4 ounces)

Cut tops from peppers; discard seeds and membranes. Cook peppers in boiling salted water for 5 minutes; drain. Arrange in a 12x7½x2-inch baking dish. In skillet cook ground pork and onion till meat is browned and onion is tender. Drain off excess fat. Season with salt and pepper. Stir in *undrained* tomatoes, uncooked rice, water, celery, chicken bouillon granules, basil, and thyme. Cover; simmer about 20 minutes or till rice is tender.

Spoon meat mixture into peppers. Cover with moisture-vapor-proof wrap. Seal, label, and freeze.

Before serving: Bake, covered, in a 350° oven about 70 minutes or till heated through. Sprinkle with cheese. Return to oven; bake, uncovered, 5 minutes more or till cheese melts. Makes 6 servings.

Meats

Oriental Pork on Rice

1 pound boneless pork, cut into thin bite-size strips
1 tablespoon cooking oil
1¼ cups water
¾ cup bias-sliced celery
1 medium onion, thinly sliced
¼ cup dry sherry
3 tablespoons soy sauce
1 clove garlic, minced
¼ teaspoon ground ginger
¼ cup cold water
2 tablespoons cornstarch
2 cups loose pack frozen broccoli, cauliflower, and carrots
½ cup sliced water chestnuts
1 4-ounce can sliced mushrooms, drained
Hot cooked rice

In 10-inch skillet brown meat strips in hot oil. Add water, celery, onion, sherry, soy sauce, garlic, and ginger. Bring to boiling; reduce heat and simmer, covered, for 40 minutes.

Combine cold water and cornstarch; add to skillet mixture. Cook and stir till thickened and bubbly. Cook and stir 1 to 2 minutes more. Remove from heat. Stir in mixed vegetables, water chestnuts, and mushrooms. Pour into a 6-cup freezer container. Cover, seal, label, and freeze.

Before serving: In covered saucepan cook frozen mixture about 30 minutes or till heated through, stirring occasionally with fork to break apart. Serve over hot cooked rice. Makes 4 servings.

Pineapple and Pork Chops

4 pork chops, cut ¾ inch thick
2 tablespoons cooking oil
1 8-ounce can pineapple slices (juice pack)
1 tablespoon brown sugar
2 teaspoons cornstarch
1½ teaspoons instant chicken bouillon granules
¼ teaspoon ground cinnamon
2 cups cooked rice
¼ cup raisins

Trim and discard excess fat from chops. Season chops with salt and pepper. In a 10-inch skillet brown chops in hot oil. Reduce heat; cover and cook about 40 minutes or till tender. Drain off excess fat. Set chops aside. Add enough water to pan juices to measure ½ cup liquid; return to skillet. Drain pineapple, reserving juice. Halve *two* of the pineapple slices; cut up remaining pineapple and set aside.

For pineapple sauce, combine reserved pineapple juice, brown sugar, cornstarch, chicken granules, and cinnamon. Add to skillet. Cook and stir till thickened and bubbly. Cook and stir 1 to 2 minutes more. Toss together cut-up pineapple, cooked rice, and raisins. Stir in *half* of the pineapple sauce. Turn pineapple-rice mixture into a 9x9x2-inch baking pan. Top with chops. Top each chop with half of a pineapple slice. Pour remaining sauce over chops. Cover with moisture-vaporproof wrap. Seal, label, and freeze.

Before serving: Bake, covered, in a 400° oven for 1 to 1¼ hours or till heated through. Serves 4.

Polish Supper Bake

1 10-ounce package frozen chopped spinach
4 cups shredded zucchini
1 pound Polish sausage, chopped
5 slightly beaten eggs
1 cup milk
¾ cup finely crushed saltine crackers
½ cup grated Parmesan cheese
1 tablespoon dried parsley flakes
1½ teaspoons minced dried onion
½ teaspoon salt
½ teaspoon dried basil, crushed
¼ teaspoon pepper
1 cup dairy sour cream
¼ cup grated Parmesan cheese

Place frozen spinach in boiling water; return to boiling. Break up spinach; add shredded zucchini. Cover; simmer 5 minutes. Drain; press out liquid. Cook Polish sausage till lightly browned; drain. In mixing bowl combine eggs, milk, crushed saltine crackers, ½ cup grated Parmesan cheese, parsley flakes, dried onion, salt, basil, and pepper. Stir in sausage and spinach mixture. Divide sausage-vegetable mixture between two greased 10x6x2-inch baking dishes. Cover with moisture-vaporproof wrap. Seal, label, and freeze.

Before serving: Bake frozen casserole, covered, in a 350° oven for 1 hour. Uncover; top *each* casserole with ½ *cup* of the sour cream and 2 *tablespoons* of the Parmesan cheese. Bake, uncovered, 5 minutes more. Makes 2 casseroles, 4 to 6 servings each.

Meats

Sweet and Sour Franks

1 8¼-ounce can pineapple chunks
1 16-ounce package frankfurters (8 to 10), sliced into 1-inch pieces
1 medium green pepper, chopped
½ cup chopped carrot
1 clove garlic, minced
1 tablespoon cooking oil
1 cup chicken broth
¼ cup sugar
¼ cup red wine vinegar
2 teaspoons soy sauce
2 tablespoons cornstarch
½ cup water
1 3-ounce can chow mein noodles

Drain pineapple chunks, reserving ¼ cup of the syrup. In skillet cook sliced franks, green pepper, carrot, and garlic in hot oil till vegetables are tender. Stir in chicken broth, sugar, vinegar, and soy sauce. Bring to boiling. Blend cornstarch into the reserved pineapple syrup; add to frank mixture. Cook and stir till thickened and bubbly. Cook and stir 1 to 2 minutes more. Stir in pineapple. Turn frankfurter mixture into a 5- to 6-cup freezer container. Cover, seal, label, and freeze. (If desired, frankfurter mixture may be frozen in 1- or 2-cup portions.)

Before serving: In covered saucepan cook frozen frankfurter mixture with the water about 30 minutes or till heated through. (For 1- or 2-cup portions, add 2 to 4 tablespoons water as needed when reheating frozen mixture.) Serve over chow mein noodles. Serves 4.

Lentil and Ham Soup

Serve a thick and crusty slice of French bread with this hearty soup —

1 16-ounce package dry lentils (2¼ cups)
10 cups water
1 pound fully cooked ham, cubed (3 cups)
1½ cups chopped carrot
1 cup chopped celery
1 cup chopped onion
¼ cup snipped parsley
1 tablespoon instant beef bouillon granules
1 teaspoon dried marjoram, crushed
¼ teaspoon pepper
1 bay leaf

Rinse dry lentils thoroughly in cold water; drain. In a Dutch oven combine the lentils, the water, the cubed ham, chopped carrot, chopped celery, chopped onion, parsley, beef bouillon granules, marjoram, pepper, and bay leaf. Cover and simmer about 35 minutes or till lentils are tender. Remove bay leaf and discard.

Divide lentil mixture between three 5- to 6-cup freezer containers. Cover, seal, label, and freeze.

Before serving: In a covered saucepan heat each portion of frozen lentil soup over medium-low heat about 40 minutes or till soup is heated through, stirring occasionally to break apart mixture. Season to taste with salt and pepper. Makes three 5-cup portions, 4 servings each.

Apricot-Ham Patties

1 beaten egg
⅓ cup milk
¾ cup soft bread crumbs (1 slice bread)
¼ cup finely snipped dried apricots
2 tablespoons chopped onion
1 tablespoon snipped parsley
½ pound ground fully cooked ham
½ pound ground pork

In a bowl combine egg and milk. Stir in bread crumbs, dried apricots, onion, parsley, and dash *pepper.* Add ground ham and pork; mix well. With wet hands, shape meat mixture into 4 patties. Place ham patties in bottom of a 9x9x2-inch baking pan. Cover pan with moisture-vaporproof wrap. Seal, label, and freeze.

Before serving: Bake, covered, in a 400° oven for 45 minutes. Uncover, bake 15 minutes more or till patties are done. Serves 4.

Freezing Tip

Make more efficient use of your baking dishes when freezing foods. First, line the dish or pan with heavy foil. Place the food mixture in the foil-lined dish. Cover with moisture-vaporproof wrap. Freeze. When frozen solid, carefully remove the sealed-in-foil food. Seal, label, and return to freezer. Now you can use the dish or pan for other baking jobs.

Poultry

Italian Boneless Chicken

6 beaten eggs
2 cups grated Parmesan
   cheese (8 ounces)
½ cup fine dry bread crumbs
4 cups finely chopped cooked
   chicken
3 tablespoons butter *or*
   margarine
½ cup chopped green pepper
½ cup chopped onion
1 tablespoon cooking oil
2 15-ounce cans tomato sauce
1 teaspoon sugar
½ teaspoon Italian seasoning
¼ teaspoon dried basil, crushed
¼ teaspoon garlic powder
⅛ teaspoon pepper
2 cups shredded mozzarella
   cheese (8 ounces)

Combine eggs, Parmesan, and bread crumbs. Stir in chicken; mix well. With wet hands, shape mixture into sixteen ¾-inch-thick patties. In a large skillet cook patties in butter or margarine over medium-high heat 2 to 3 minutes per side or till browned. Drain patties; arrange in two 10x6x2-inch baking dishes. Cook green pepper and onion in hot oil till tender. Remove from heat. Add ½ cup *water* and remaining ingredients *except* mozzarella. Spoon sauce mixture over patties; sprinkle with mozzarella cheese. Cover each casserole with moisture-vaporproof wrap. Seal, label, and freeze.

Before serving: Bake frozen casserole, covered, in a 400° oven for 50 minutes. Uncover and bake 20 minutes more or till heated through. Makes 2 casseroles, 4 or 5 servings each.

Chicken and Cream Cheese Sandwiches

1 3-ounce package cream
   cheese, softened
1 teaspoon lemon juice
8 slices whole wheat *or* rye
   bread
1 5-ounce can boned chicken
   or turkey, drained
2 tablespoons chopped pitted
   ripe olives
2 teaspoons finely chopped
   onion
   Butter *or* margarine, softened
   Lettuce leaves (optional)
   Thinly sliced tomatoes
   (optional)
   Alfalfa *or* bean sprouts
   (optional)

In mixing bowl beat cream cheese and lemon juice till well blended. Spread cream cheese mixture on one side of 4 of the bread slices. Combine the canned chicken or turkey, chopped ripe olives, and the onion. Spoon chicken mixture atop cream cheese mixture. Spread remaining bread slices with butter or margarine on one side; place, buttered side down, atop chicken mixture. Wrap with moisture-vaporproof wrap. Seal, label, and freeze.

Before serving: Thaw sandwiches. If desired, add lettuce leaves, tomato slices, and alfalfa or bean sprouts to sandwiches. Makes 4 servings.

Elegant Chicken with Grapes

2 whole large chicken breasts,
   halved lengthwise
2 tablespoons butter *or*
   margarine
3 tablespoons dry white wine
¼ cup orange marmalade
1 teaspoon snipped parsley
1 cup seeded red grapes *or*
   seedless green grapes,
   halved

Season chicken with salt. In skillet brown chicken slowly in hot butter or margarine for 5 to 10 minutes, turning frequently. Spoon wine over chicken. Cover and simmer 5 minutes. Remove from heat. Remove chicken pieces to a 10x6x2-inch baking dish.

If necessary, skim off fat from pan juices. Stir in orange marmalade and parsley. Stir in grapes. Pour over chicken pieces in baking dish. Cover with moisture-vaporproof wrap. Seal, label, and freeze.

Before serving: Bake, covered, in a 375° oven about 55 minutes or till chicken is done. Remove chicken to serving platter. Keep warm. Measure juices; pour into saucepan. Boil about 5 minutes or till reduced to ½ cup. Serve chicken topped with grape sauce. Makes 4 servings.

*Chicken and Cream Cheese
Sandwiches
Italian Boneless Chicken
Elegant Chicken with Grapes*

Poultry

Creamy Chicken and Vegetables

⅓ cup chopped onion
2 tablespoons butter *or* margarine
2 tablespoons all-purpose flour
¾ teaspoon salt
2¼ cups milk
1 3-ounce package cream cheese, cut up
1 10-ounce package frozen peas and carrots
2 cups chopped cooked chicken *or* turkey
2 tablespoons dry white wine
Toast points *or* toasted English muffins

In medium saucepan cook chopped onion in butter or margarine till tender. Stir in flour and salt. Add milk all at once. Cook and stir till mixture is thickened and bubbly. Cook and stir 1 to 2 minutes more. Stir in cut-up cream cheese till melted. Remove from heat.

Add frozen mixed vegetables, cooked chicken or turkey, and white wine to cooked mixture; stir till well combined. Turn mixture into a 5-cup freezer container. Cover, seal, label, and freeze.

Before serving: In saucepan cook frozen mixture till heated through, stirring occasionally. Serve at once over toast points or toasted English muffins. Makes 4 servings.

Tarragon Chicken in Foil

Prepare, wrap, and freeze these individual chicken main dishes. They'll be ready to take from freezer to oven and bake when one serving is all you need —

2 whole large chicken breasts, halved lengthwise
¼ cup chopped onion
2 tablespoons butter *or* margarine
2 cups frozen peas
2 tablespoons dry white wine
1 teaspoon instant chicken bouillon granules
½ teaspoon dried tarragon, crushed

In skillet cook chicken and onion in butter or margarine till chicken is browned and onion is tender. Remove chicken from pan, reserving onion. Place each chicken piece on double-layered 12x12-inch piece of foil. Turn up edges of foil.

Spoon ½ cup frozen peas around each chicken piece. Stir dry white wine, chicken bouillon granules, and tarragon into the cooked onion; spoon over chicken pieces. Bring up sides of foil, folding twice to seal; seal ends. Label and freeze.

Before serving: Place desired number of frozen foil packages on a baking sheet. Bake in a 375° oven about 50 minutes or till chicken is tender. Remove from foil packets to serve. Makes 4 foil packets, 1 serving each.

Rolled Turkey Tortillas

¼ cup chopped onion
1 clove garlic, minced
1 tablespoon butter *or* margarine
1 5-ounce can boned turkey, drained and chopped
2 canned green chili peppers, rinsed, seeded, and chopped
½ of a 7½-ounce can (½ cup) tomatoes, cut up
⅓ cup tomato paste
¼ teaspoon salt
¼ teaspoon ground cumin
4 large flour tortillas
1 cup shredded cheddar cheese (4 ounces)
1 small avocado, seeded, peeled, and chopped
Cooking oil
Dairy sour cream
Sliced green onion

In saucepan cook onion and garlic in butter or margarine till onion is tender. Remove from heat. Stir in turkey, chili peppers, *undrained* tomatoes, tomato paste, salt, and cumin. Spoon about ⅓ cup turkey mixture onto each tortilla near edge. Top each with *2 tablespoons* shredded cheese and ¼ of the chopped avocado; roll up. Place filled tortillas, seam side down, in a greased 13x9x2-inch baking pan. Brush tortillas lightly with cooking oil; sprinkle with remaining cheese. Cover with moisture-vaporproof wrap. Seal, label, and freeze.

Before serving: Bake, uncovered, in a 350° oven for 40 to 45 minutes or till heated through. Serve hot tortillas topped with a dollop of sour cream. Sprinkle with green onion. Makes 4 servings.

Fish

Fish and Fried Rice Bake

1 pound fresh or frozen fish
  fillets
¼ cup chopped celery
¼ cup chopped green pepper
¼ cup sliced green onion
2 tablespoons butter or
  margarine
2 teaspoons cornstarch
⅓ cup water
1 tablespoon soy sauce
1 tablespoon honey
1 teaspoon vinegar
1 11-ounce can fried rice
  Soy sauce (optional)

If frozen, let fish stand at room temperature 20 minutes. Cut fish into 1-inch cubes. Meanwhile, in large saucepan cook the chopped celery, chopped green pepper, and sliced green onion in butter or margarine till tender. Stir in cornstarch. Add water, 1 tablespoon soy sauce, honey, and vinegar. Cook and stir till thickened and bubbly. Cook and stir 1 to 2 minutes more.

Stir the can of fried rice and the cubed fish into the thickened mixture. Turn mixture into a 10x6x2-inch baking dish. Cover with moisture-vaporproof wrap. Seal, label, and freeze.

Before serving: Bake, covered, in a 375° oven about 1¼ hours or till fish flakes easily when tested with a fork. Pass soy sauce, if desired. Makes 4 servings.

Creamy Tuna Casserole

1½ cups corkscrew or elbow
  macaroni
½ cup chopped onion
⅓ cup chopped green pepper
2 tablespoons butter or
  margarine
1 12½-ounce can tuna, drained
  and flaked
1 10¾-ounce can condensed
  cream of mushroom soup
1 cup shredded Swiss cheese
  (4 ounces)
⅔ cup milk
1 4-ounce can mushroom
  stems and pieces, drained
⅓ cup chopped peanuts

Cook the corkscrew or elbow macaroni according to package directions except omit the salt; drain. In saucepan cook the chopped onion and chopped green pepper in butter or margarine till tender. Remove from heat. Stir in tuna, condensed cream of mushroom soup, shredded Swiss cheese, milk, and mushroom stems and pieces. Stir in the cooked macaroni.

Turn the macaroni-tuna mixture into a 1½-quart casserole. Cover with moisture-vaporproof wrap. Seal, label, and freeze.

Before serving: Bake, covered, in a 400° oven about 1¼ hours or till heated through. Sprinkle the chopped peanuts around edge of casserole. Bake 5 minutes more. Makes 6 servings.

Salmon and Cheese Sandwiches

Take a frozen sandwich from the freezer in the morning to carry to work or school. It will be thawed and ready to eat by lunch —

1 7¾-ounce can salmon
1 4-ounce container whipped
  cream cheese with chives
⅓ cup shredded cheddar
  cheese
¼ cup sweet pickle relish
  Butter or margarine
8 slices whole wheat bread

Drain salmon; flake salmon, removing skin and bones. Combine with cheeses and pickle relish; mix well. Spread whole wheat bread slices lightly with butter or margarine on one side. Spread 4 bread slices with salmon mixture; top with remaining bread slices. Wrap with moisture-vaporproof wrap. Seal, label, and freeze.

Before serving: Thaw sandwiches. Makes 4 servings.

Microwave Reheating

To reheat a frozen mixture, cook in a nonmetal baking dish in a counter-top microwave oven on high power. Micro-cook a 2-cup mixture for 9 to 10 minutes, a 4-cup mixture for 22 to 24 minutes, and a 6-cup mixture for 33 to 35 minutes. Stir the mixture twice during cooking and just before serving.

Seafood and Cheese

Shrimp and Cheese Casserole

 1 10-ounce package frozen chopped spinach
 1 tablespoon butter *or* margarine
 1 tablespoon all-purpose flour
 ¼ teaspoon dried dillweed
 ½ cup milk
 1 tablespoon dry sherry
 ½ cup cream-style cottage cheese
 ½ cup shredded mozzarella cheese (2 ounces)
 2 4½-ounce cans shrimp, drained and rinsed
 1 cup cooked noodles
 ¾ cup soft rye bread crumbs (1 slice)
 1 tablespoon butter *or* margarine, melted

Cook spinach according to package directions; drain well. In saucepan melt 1 tablespoon butter or margarine. Stir in flour and dillweed till well blended. Add milk and sherry all at once. Cook and stir till thickened and bubbly. Cook and stir 1 to 2 minutes more. Stir in cottage cheese and mozzarella cheese. Add spinach, shrimp, and noodles; toss lightly to mix.

Spoon mixture into a 10x6x2-inch baking dish. Toss bread crumbs with the 1 tablespoon melted butter or margarine; sprinkle around edge of casserole. Cover with moisture-vaporproof wrap. Seal, label, and freeze.

Before serving: Bake, uncovered, in a 400° oven about 45 minutes or till bubbly. Makes 4 servings.

Stuffed Cabbage Rolls with Curry Sauce

 4 cups cooked rice
 ½ cup chopped green onion
 ½ cup shredded carrot
 ½ cup chopped peanuts
 ⅓ cup grated Parmesan cheese
 ⅓ cup finely chopped chutney
 2 tablespoons cooking oil
 1 clove garlic, minced
 ¼ teaspoon salt
 ⅛ teaspoon pepper
 12 large cabbage leaves
 ¼ cup water
 2 tablespoons butter
 2 tablespoons all-purpose flour
 1½ to 2 teaspoons curry powder
 ¼ teaspoon salt
 1⅓ cups milk
 1 cup shredded Monterey Jack *or* mozzarella cheese
 2 tablespoons snipped parsley

In bowl combine cooked rice, green onion, carrot, peanuts, Parmesan cheese, chutney, cooking oil, garlic, ¼ teaspoon salt, and pepper; mix well. Set aside.

Cut about 2 inches of the heavy vein out of the cabbage leaves. Immerse leaves in boiling water about 3 minutes or just till limp; drain. Sprinkle leaves generously with salt. Place a *scant ½ cup* of the rice-vegetable mixture in the center of each leaf; fold in sides. Fold ends so they overlap rice mixture.

Place, seam side down, in 12x7½x2-inch baking dish. Cover with moisture-vaporproof wrap. Seal, label, and freeze.

Before serving: Pour the ¼ cup water into baking dish. Bake, covered, in a 350° oven about 1 hour and 20 minutes or till heated through.

Meanwhile, for sauce, in saucepan melt butter. Stir in flour, curry powder, and the ¼ teaspoon salt. Add milk all at once. Cook and stir over medium heat till thickened and bubbly. Cook and stir 1 to 2 minutes more. Add shredded cheese, stirring till cheese is melted. Pass sauce with baked cabbage rolls. Sprinkle with parsley. Makes 6 servings.

Curried Scallop Bake

 ¾ pound fresh *or* frozen scallops
 1 10¾-ounce can condensed cream of celery soup
 ¼ cup milk
 3 tablespoons dry white wine
 1 tablespoon chopped onion
 1 tablespoon snipped parsley
 2 to 3 teaspoons curry powder
 ¼ teaspoon paprika
 1 3-ounce package cream cheese, cut up
 4 ounces spaghetti, broken, cooked, and drained

Thaw scallops, if frozen. Combine celery soup, milk, wine, onion, snipped parsley, curry powder, and paprika. Bring to boiling, stirring occasionally. Stir in cream cheese; cook and stir till melted.

Halve any large scallops; stir into soup mixture. Simmer, covered, 1 minute. Spoon cooked spaghetti into 10x6x2-inch baking dish. Top with scallop mixture. Cover with moisture-vaporproof wrap. Seal, label, and freeze.

Before serving: Bake, covered, in 350° oven about 1 hour and 20 minutes or till done. Serves 4.

Cheese

Cheese Custard Puffs

Prepare and freeze these elegant individual cheese puffs. They'll be ready when unexpected guests drop in for a meal —

6 tablespoons butter *or* margarine
⅓ cup all-purpose flour
2 cups milk
3 cups shredded American cheese (12 ounces)
6 eggs
½ teaspoon cream of tartar

In saucepan melt butter or margarine. Stir in flour. Add milk all at once. Cook and stir till thickened and bubbly. Cook and stir 1 or 2 minutes more. Add the shredded American cheese; stir till melted. Remove from heat.

Separate eggs, beat yolks till thick and lemon-colored. Gradually stir cheese mixture into yolks; cool. Using clean beaters, in large mixer bowl beat egg whites with cream of tartar till stiff peaks form (tips stand straight). Fold yolk mixture into whites. Pour mixture into 8 ungreased 1-cup soufflé dishes. Cover with moisture-vaporproof wrap. Seal, label, and freeze.

Before serving: Set the desired number of individual frozen cheese puffs in a shallow baking pan filled with ½ inch hot water. Bake, uncovered, in a 300° oven about 1¼ hours. Makes 8 servings.

Cheese-Stuffed Whole Wheat Ravioli

1 beaten egg
½ cup ricotta cheese
½ cup shredded mozzarella cheese (2 ounces)
⅓ cup grated Parmesan cheese
¼ cup pine nuts *or* almonds
¼ cup snipped parsley
½ teaspoon dried marjoram, crushed
½ cup whole wheat flour
1 beaten egg
3 tablespoons water
½ teaspoon cooking oil
¾ cup all-purpose flour
1 28-ounce can tomatoes, finely cut up
¾ cup sliced celery
¾ cup finely chopped carrot
1 teaspoon sugar
½ teaspoon dried marjoram, crushed
1 tablespoon cold water
2 teaspoons cornstarch
1 tablespoon cooking oil
¼ cup grated Parmesan cheese

For filling, in mixing bowl combine 1 egg, ricotta cheese, mozzarella cheese, ⅓ cup Parmesan cheese, pine nuts, parsley, and ½ teaspoon marjoram. Set aside.

For pasta, in mixing bowl stir together whole wheat flour and ¼ teaspoon *salt*. Make a well in center. Combine 1 egg, 3 tablespoons water, and ½ teaspoon cooking oil. Add to whole wheat flour; mix well. Add as much all-purpose flour as you can stir in with a spoon. On lightly floured surface knead dough till elastic (8 to 10 minutes). Cover and let rest 10 minutes.

Roll dough to a 16x12-inch rectangle or 32x6-inch rectangle if using pasta machine. (If dough becomes too elastic during rolling, cover and let rest 5 minutes.) Using sharp knife or fluted pastry wheel, cut dough into 2-inch squares.

Place *1 rounded teaspoon* filling on one square. Top with second square; press firmly with tines of fork to seal edges. Repeat with remaining dough and filling. Wrap in moisture-vaporproof wrap. Seal, label, and freeze.

For sauce, in large saucepan combine *undrained* tomatoes, celery, carrot, sugar, ½ teaspoon marjoram, ½ teaspoon *salt,* and ⅛ teaspoon *pepper.* Bring to boiling; reduce heat. Cover and boil gently about 15 minutes or till vegetables are tender, stirring occasionally.

To blender or food processor bowl add *1½ cups* of the tomato mixture. Cover and blend till smooth. Combine the 1 tablespoon cold water and cornstarch; add to blender. Cover and blend till combined. Return mixture to saucepan. Cook and stir till thickened and bubbly. Cook 1 to 2 minutes more. Cool; pour into freezer container. Cover, seal, label, and freeze.

Before serving: Place frozen sauce in saucepan; cook over low heat till heated through. Meanwhile, in Dutch oven bring 3 quarts *water* and 1 tablespoon *salt* to boiling. Add the 1 tablespoon cooking oil. Add frozen filled ravioli, a few at a time. Reduce heat; continue boiling gently for 5 to 8 minutes; or till pasta is tender but slightly firm. Drain. *Do not rinse.* Transfer to a warm serving dish. Top with sauce and the ¼ cup Parmesan cheese. Serve immediately. Serves 4.

Freezer Guide

Use your freezer to store all types of make-ahead foods. Keep an inventory of these frozen items and use foods within their recommended storage times, using the chart below as a guide.

Here are a few tips to help you with make-ahead recipe selection, food preparation, and serving directions:

- Don't overcook foods.
- Package foods to be frozen properly. Use freezer containers or moisture-vaporproof wrap such as freezer paper, heavy foil, or plastic bags when packaging foods for the freezer. Or, cover containers with a lid and fix freezer tape around the edges to make a leak-proof seal. Allow headspace (room

for food to expand) when packing liquid or semiliquid foods in a container.
- Use cooking oil, butter or margarine, and other fats sparingly in sauces. They don't blend in well when reheated. Stirring may help during reheating.
- Freeze most casseroles before baking, especially when ingredi-

Food	Preparation for Freezing	How to Serve	Storage Time
Breads Biscuits and muffins	Bake as usual; cool. Seal in a freezer container or wrap with moisture-vaporproof wrap; seal and label.	Thaw in package at room temperature 1 hour or reheat in foil in a 300° oven about 20 minutes.	2 months
Yeast breads and rolls	Bake as usual; cool. Wrap with moisture-vaporproof wrap. Seal and label.	Thaw at room temperature. Or, reheat in foil in a 300° oven about 40 minutes for a loaf and 15 minutes for rolls.	4 to 8 months
Cakes General	Bake cake or cupcakes as usual. Remove from pan; cool thoroughly. (If cake is frosted, freeze it before wrapping.) Wrap with moisture-vaporproof wrap; seal and label. If desired, place in a sturdy container. (Unfrosted cakes and cupcakes freeze better; frosted and filled cakes may become soggy.)	Thaw in wrapping at room temperature (allow 2 to 3 hours for a large cake, 1 hour for layers, and about 40 minutes for cupcakes). Thaw frosted or filled cakes loosely covered in the refrigerator.	6 months
Cookies Unbaked, general	Pack unbaked dough in freezer containers; seal and label. Not recommended for freezing: Meringue-type cookies.	Thaw in container at room temperature till dough is soft. Bake as usual.	6 months
Refrigerator cookies	Shape unbaked dough into a roll. Wrap in moisture-vaporproof wrap.	Thaw slightly at room temperature. Slice roll; bake as usual.	6 months
Baked, general	Bake as usual; cool. Pack in freezer containers. Seal and label.	Thaw in package at room temperature.	6 to 12 months
Pies Fruit, general two-crust	Unbaked: Treat light-colored fruits with ascorbic acid color keeper to prevent darkening. Prepare pie as usual; do not slit top crust. Use freezer-to-oven pie plate. Cover with inverted paper plate to protect crust. Wrap with moisture-vaporproof wrap; seal and label.	Unwrap; cut vent holes in top crust. Cover edge of crust with foil. Without thawing, bake in a 450° oven for 15 minutes, then in a 375° oven for 15 minutes. Uncover edge and bake about 30 to 35 minutes longer or till done. (Bake juicy pies on baking sheet.)	3 months

ents are cooked. Exceptions to this include dishes that contain uncooked rice, raw vegetables, or uncooked meat that has been frozen and thawed.

● Cool cooked foods quickly before wrapping and placing in the freezer. Place the pan of hot cooked food in ice water to cool to room temperature.

● Be sure to label packages with their contents and the date. Use foods within the suggested storage time, following the guidelines on the chart below.

● Keep your freezer set at 0°F. or lower for maximum food preservation.

● Add crumb toppers to casseroles at reheating time.

● For "wet" vegetables such as spinach, drain well after cooking, pressing out any excess moisture by using several layers of paper toweling.

● Prepare frozen foods for serving following the directions in the tables below. Or, check your microwave oven cook book for thawing and reheating directions.

Food	Preparation for Freezing	How to Serve	Storage Time
Pies (cont'd)	Baked: Bake as usual in a glass or metal pie plate. Cool and package as above for unbaked pies.	Thaw in package at room temperature or covered with foil in a 300° oven.	2 to 3 months
Main Dishes Casseroles: Poultry, fish, or meat with vegetables or pasta	Prepare main dishes slightly undercooked and season lightly; add more seasoning when reheating, if desired. Cool mixture quickly. Turn into a freezer container or freezer-to-oven casserole dish. Cover tightly with moisture-vaporproof wrap or container lid. Seal and label.	If frozen in a freezer-to-oven casserole, bake, covered, in a 400° oven for half of baking time; uncover for second half of baking time. Allow about 1 hour for pints, 1¾ hours for quarts, or bake till hot.	
Meatballs with tomato-type spaghetti sauce	Cook till done; cool quickly. Ladle into freezer jars or containers, allowing headspace (don't use metal or foil for acidic foods). Seal and label.	Heat in a heavy saucepan over low heat, stirring frequently, or in the top of a double boiler, stirring occasionally. Or, defrost overnight in the refrigerator. Heat.	3 months
Stews and soups	Select vegetables that freeze well. Omit potatoes. Green pepper and garlic become more intense in flavor. Omit salt and thickening if stew is to be kept longer than 2 months. Do not completely cook vegetables. Cool soup or stew mixture quickly; turn into a freezer container. Cover tightly. Seal and label.	Heat from the frozen state in a heavy saucepan over low heat. Separate with a fork during thawing. Do not overcook. Season and thicken heated stew before serving.	6 months
Sandwiches	These freeze well: Cream cheese, chopped hard-cooked egg, meat, poultry, tuna, salmon, and peanut butter. Spread bread with softened butter or margarine; fill. Wrap tightly. Seal and label. Not recommended: Lettuce, celery, tomatoes, cucumber, watercress, jelly, and mayonnaise.	Thaw sandwiches in wrapping at room temperature about 3 hours.	1 month

Side Dishes

Fresh-baked breads, savory vegetable casseroles, and tasty gelatin salads — all can be served with little last-minute preparation using recipes you'll find in this chapter.

After advance preparation, these side dishes are stored in the refrigerator, in the freezer, or on your pantry shelf. Then, they're on call to round out a meal when needed.

Turn to this chapter of recipes when you want to serve something other than store-bought bread or vegetables straight from a can. Side dish recipes you can choose from include marinated vegetables, vegetable salads, gelatin salads, and vegetable casseroles. There's also muffin batter that is refrigerated ready-to-bake, homemade frozen bread dough that only needs to rise before baking, even frozen rolls that just need to brown before serving.

*Cauliflower and Cheese Bake
(see recipe, page 65)
Layered Cranberry-Apple
Mold (see recipe, page 69)
Dutch Cucumbers in Sour
Cream (see recipe, page 63)
Twice-Baked Cheesy Potatoes
(see recipe, page 63)*

Vegetables

Vegetable-Wine Sauce

  8 pounds tomatoes, peeled, cored, and cut up (about 24 medium)
1½ cups chopped onion
1½ cups chopped carrot
  1 cup chopped green pepper
  1 cup snipped parsley
  4 cloves garlic, minced
  2 tablespoons snipped fresh basil or 2 teaspoons dried basil, crushed
  4 teaspoons salt
  1 tablespoon snipped fresh oregano or 1 teaspoon dried oregano, crushed
  2 teaspoons sugar
  ⅛ teaspoon ground red pepper
  ½ medium eggplant, peeled and cubed (about 3 cups)
  1 cup dry red wine
    Hot cooked pasta

In large kettle or Dutch oven combine tomatoes, onion, carrot, green pepper, parsley, garlic, basil, salt, oregano, sugar, and red pepper. Bring to boiling; reduce heat. Boil gently, uncovered, for 1½ to 1¾ hours or till very thick, stirring occasionally. Add eggplant and wine to tomato mixture. Cook for 10 to 15 minutes more or till sauce is of desired consistency; stir occasionally. Cool.

Ladle the sauce into six 2-cup freezer containers. Cover, seal, label, and freeze.

Before serving: Place desired amount of frozen sauce in saucepan. Bring the mixture to boiling, stirring occasionally. Serve the hot sauce over hot cooked pasta. Makes 12 cups.

Vegetable Vinaigrette

  1 pint fresh brussels sprouts or one 10-ounce package frozen brussels sprouts
  2 cups fresh or frozen cauliflower flowerets
  ½ cup salad oil
  3 tablespoons white wine vinegar
  3 tablespoons lemon juice
  ¾ teaspoon salt
  ¾ teaspoon dry mustard
  ½ teaspoon sugar
  4 to 6 tomatoes
    Romaine leaves
    Sieved hard-cooked egg (optional)
    Snipped parsley (optional)

Trim stems slightly from fresh brussels sprouts. Remove discolored leaves, wash, and halve sprouts. Place fresh sprouts and cauliflower flowerets in steamer rack over boiling water. Cover and steam 7 to 10 minutes or till crisp-tender. (For frozen brussels sprouts and cauliflower flowerets, cook according to package directions till crisp-tender.) Drain. Place vegetables in a glass bowl.

For dressing, in a screw-top jar combine salad oil, vinegar, lemon juice, salt, mustard, and sugar; cover and shake well. Pour dressing over vegetables. Toss lightly to coat. Cover tightly and refrigerate for 3 to 24 hours.

To make tomato shells, cut small slice from top of each tomato. Remove core. Scoop out seeds, leaving a ½-inch-thick shell. Invert; cover and chill.

Before serving: Place tomato shells on romaine-lined serving plates. Drain marinade from vegetables. Spoon vegetables into tomato shells. If desired, sprinkle sieved hard-cooked egg and snipped parsley atop. Makes 4 to 6 servings.

Green Beans in Chutney Marinade

  2 cups fresh green beans cut into 1-inch pieces or one 9-ounce package frozen cut green beans
  ¼ cup chopped chutney
  2 tablespoons chopped celery
  2 tablespoons sliced green onion
  3 tablespoons olive oil or salad oil
  2 tablespoons sugar
  2 tablespoons lemon juice
  ½ small clove garlic, minced
  ¼ teaspoon salt
  2 tablespoons coarsely chopped walnuts

In medium saucepan cook fresh beans, uncovered, in boiling salted water about 20 minutes or till crisp-tender. (Or, cook frozen beans according to package directions till crisp-tender.) Drain. Combine beans, chutney, celery, and green onion. In a small deep bowl combine olive or salad oil, sugar, lemon juice, garlic, and salt; beat with rotary beater till slightly thickened. Add oil mixture to bean mixture; mix well. Cover and refrigerate for 3 to 24 hours.

Before serving: Sprinkle with walnuts. Makes 6 servings.

Vegetables

Dutch Cucumbers in Sour Cream

Pictured on pages 60 and 61 —

  2 medium cucumbers
  1 large onion, sliced and
      separated into rings
1½ teaspoons salt
  ¾ cup water
  ¾ cup vinegar
  1 teaspoon sugar
  ½ cup dairy sour cream
  1 teaspoon dillseed
  1 to 2 drops bottled hot pepper
      sauce
      Dash freshly ground pepper
      Cucumber peel (optional)

Peel *one* of the cucumbers. Thinly slice both cucumbers. In bowl combine cucumbers, onion, and the salt. Stir together water, vinegar, and sugar; pour over cucumber-onion mixture. Let mixture stand at room temperature for 1 hour; drain well. Cover and refrigerate for 3 to 24 hours.

For dressing, combine the sour cream, dillseed, bottled hot pepper sauce, and freshly ground pepper. Cover and refrigerate for 3 to 24 hours.

Before serving: Pour sour cream dressing over cucumber mixture. Toss gently with sliced cucumbers and onions. Garnish with cucumber peel, if desired. Makes 6 servings.

Twice-Baked Cheesy Potatoes

Pictured on pages 60 and 61 —

  4 medium baking potatoes
  2 tablespoons butter
  ½ cup dairy sour cream
  ½ cup shredded American
      cheese (2 ounces)
  2 tablespoons thinly sliced
      green onion

Scrub potatoes thoroughly and prick with fork. Bake in 425° oven for 40 to 60 minutes or till done. Cut a lengthwise slice from the top of each potato; discard skin from slice. Scoop out the inside of each potato, leaving ½-inch shell. Set shells aside; mash potato. Add butter to potato. Beat in sour cream. Season with ½ teaspoon *salt* and ⅛ teaspoon *pepper*. Stir in cheese and green onion. Spoon or pipe mashed potato mixture into potato shells. Place in a 10x6x2-inch baking dish. Cover and refrigerate for 2 to 24 hours. (*Or,* wrap in moisture-vaporproof wrap; seal, label, and freeze.)

Before serving: Bake, uncovered, in 425° oven about 35 minutes or till lightly browned. (*Or,* bake frozen potatoes 1 hour.) Sprinkle with paprika, if desired. Serves 4.

● **Microwave directions:** Scrub potatoes; prick with fork. Place in counter-top microwave oven on paper toweling, leaving at least 1 inch between potatoes. Micro-cook, uncovered, on high power for 13 to 15 minutes or till done. Halfway through cooking time, rearrange and turn potatoes.

Prepare potato shells and mashed potato mixture as directed. Fill potato shells. Place in a 10x6x2-inch nonmetal baking dish. Cover and refrigerate as directed. Before serving, micro-cook, uncovered, on high power about 10 minutes or till potatoes are heated through, rearranging potatoes twice. (*Or,* micro-cook frozen potatoes for 15 to 18 minutes or till heated through.) Sprinkle with paprika, if desired.

Corn-Mushroom Bake

  ¼ cup all-purpose flour
  1 16-ounce can cream-style
      corn
  1 3-ounce package cream
      cheese, cut up
  ½ teaspoon onion salt
  1 16-ounce can whole kernel
      corn, drained
  1 6-ounce can sliced
      mushrooms, drained
  ½ cup shredded Swiss cheese
1½ cups soft rye bread crumbs
  2 tablespoons butter, melted

In saucepan stir flour into cream-style corn. Add cream cheese and onion salt; cook and stir till cheese melts. Stir whole kernel corn, mushrooms, and Swiss cheese into hot mixture. Pour into a 1½-quart casserole. Cover and refrigerate for 3 to 24 hours.

Before serving: Bake casserole, covered, in a 400° oven about 20 minutes. Combine bread crumbs and melted butter or margarine; sprinkle over casserole. Bake, uncovered, 30 minutes more. Makes 6 to 8 servings.

Vegetables

Golden Squash and Carrot Bisque

3 medium yellow summer squash, sliced (3 cups)
1 13¾-ounce can (1¾ cups) chicken broth
2 medium carrots, sliced (1 cup)
1 medium onion, chopped (½ cup)
½ teaspoon salt
1 13-ounce can (1⅔ cups) evaporated milk
   Snipped parsley

In medium saucepan combine squash, broth, carrots, onion, and salt. Cook, covered, 15 to 20 minutes or till carrots are just tender. Turn into blender container; cover and blend till smooth. Stir in evaporated milk. Cover and refrigerate for 3 to 24 hours.

Before serving: Serve cold. Sprinkle each serving with snipped parsley. Makes 6 servings.

● **Microwave directions:** In 2-quart nonmetal casserole combine squash, carrot, and onion; sprinkle with the salt. Cook, covered, in counter-top microwave oven on high power about 15 minutes or till vegetables are tender, stirring once. In blender container combine cooked vegetables and chicken broth; cover and blend till smooth. Stir in evaporated milk. Return to casserole; cover and refrigerate for 3 to 24 hours. Serve cold. Sprinkle each serving with snipped parsley.

Carrot Pudding

8 carrots, sliced
2 medium potatoes, peeled and cubed
1 egg
2 tablespoons dairy sour cream (optional)
2 tablespoons finely shredded onion
½ teaspoon salt
¼ teaspoon pepper
2 ounces cheddar cheese, cut into small cubes (½ cup)
1 tablespoon butter or margarine
   Halved orange slices (optional)

Cook carrots, covered, in boiling salted water for 10 minutes. Add potatoes; cook, covered, 10 to 15 minutes longer. Drain vegetables; mash. Add egg, dairy sour cream, if desired, shredded onion, salt, and pepper. Beat till well blended. Stir in cheddar cheese. Spoon mixture into a 1½-quart casserole. Cover and refrigerate for 3 to 24 hours.

Before serving: Bake, uncovered, in a 350° oven about 40 minutes. Dot the top of the mixture with butter or margarine; place the uncovered casserole under broiler 5 inches from heat for 3 minutes or till the top is golden brown. Let stand 5 minutes before serving. If desired, garnish the casserole with halved orange slices. Makes 6 to 8 servings.

Carrot-Cauliflower Cheese Pie

2 cups herb-seasoned croutons, finely crushed
¼ cup butter or margarine, melted
1 cup chopped onion
1 clove garlic, minced
2 tablespoons butter or margarine
½ teaspoon dried savory, crushed
½ teaspoon dried oregano, crushed
¼ teaspoon salt
   Dash pepper
4 cups cauliflower flowerets
½ cup sliced carrot
1½ cups shredded cheddar cheese (6 ounces)
2 slightly beaten eggs
¼ cup milk

For crust, combine crushed croutons and the ¼ cup melted butter or margarine; press into 9-inch pie plate. Bake in 375° oven for 8 to 10 minutes or till golden. Set aside.

In saucepan cook onion and garlic in the 2 tablespoons butter till onion is tender but not brown. Add savory, oregano, salt, and pepper. Stir in cauliflower and carrot. Cook, covered, over low heat for 10 to 15 minutes or till vegetables are crisp-tender. Sprinkle ¾ *cup* of the shredded cheese over baked crust; spoon vegetable mixture atop. Cover and refrigerate for 3 to 24 hours.

Before serving: Combine eggs and milk. Pour over vegetables in crust. Bake in 375° oven for 35 minutes. Top with the remaining cheese; bake 5 to 10 minutes more or till set. Serves 6 to 8.

Vegetables

Cauliflower and Cheese Bake

Pictured on pages 60 and 61 —

2 10-ounce packages frozen
    cauliflower
1 10¾-ounce can condensed
    cream of onion soup
1 cup shredded cheddar
    cheese (4 ounces)
½ cup shredded carrot
¼ cup milk
1 tablespoon snipped parsley
½ teaspoon dried basil, crushed
    Dash pepper
½ of an 8-ounce package flaky
    dinner rolls

Cook cauliflower according to package directions just till tender; drain well. Halve any large pieces. Arrange cauliflower in a 1½-quart casserole.

In a mixing bowl stir together condensed onion soup, shredded cheddar cheese, shredded carrot, milk, snipped parsley, basil, and pepper. Pour over the cooked cauliflower. Cover and refrigerate for 3 to 24 hours.

Before serving: Bake, uncovered, in 350° oven for 25 minutes. Separate flaky dinner rolls; snip each roll into quarters. Arrange roll quarters around edges of baking dish. Bake 20 to 25 minutes more or till rolls are golden. Makes 8 servings.

Broccoli-Onion Bake

1 pound fresh broccoli *or* two
    10-ounce packages frozen
    cut broccoli
3 medium onions, cut into
    wedges, *or* 2 cups frozen
    small whole onions
2 tablespoons butter *or*
    margarine
2 tablespoons all-purpose flour
¼ teaspoon salt
    Dash pepper
1¼ cups milk
1 3-ounce package cream
    cheese, cut up
½ cup shredded American
    cheese (2 ounces)
1 tablespoon butter *or*
    margarine
¾ cup soft bread crumbs

Cut fresh broccoli lengthwise into spears, then into 1-inch pieces. Cook fresh or frozen broccoli in boiling salted water just till tender. Drain. Cook fresh or frozen onions in boiling salted water just till tender; drain.

In saucepan melt the 2 tablespoons butter or margarine. Stir in flour, salt, and pepper. Add milk all at once. Cook and stir till thickened and bubbly. Cook and stir 1 to 2 minutes more. Reduce heat; stir in cheeses.

Place broccoli and onions in a 1-quart casserole. Pour sauce atop; mix lightly. Cover and refrigerate for 3 to 24 hours.

Before serving: Bake, covered, in 350° oven about 30 minutes. Melt 1 tablespoon butter or margarine; toss with crumbs. Sprinkle crumb mixture atop casserole. Bake, uncovered, 35 minutes more or till heated through. Serves 6.

French Onion Casserole

4 medium onions, sliced
3 tablespoons butter *or*
    margarine
2 tablespoons all-purpose flour
    Dash pepper
1 cup hot water
¼ cup dry sherry
1½ teaspoons instant beef
    bouillon granules
¾ cup croutons
1 tablespoon butter *or*
    margarine, melted
¼ cup shredded Swiss cheese
    (1 ounce)
2 tablespoons grated
    Parmesan cheese

In covered saucepan cook onions in the 3 tablespoons butter or margarine for 5 to 10 minutes or till tender. Stir in flour and pepper. Add water, sherry, and bouillon granules to onion mixture. Cook and stir till thickened and bubbly. Cook and stir 1 to 2 minutes more. Turn mixture into a 1-quart casserole. Cover and refrigerate for 3 to 24 hours.

Before serving: Bake casserole, covered, in 350° oven for 30 minutes. Toss croutons with melted butter or margarine; sprinkle over casserole. Sprinkle Swiss cheese and Parmesan cheese atop. Bake, uncovered, for 5 to 10 minutes more. Makes 4 servings.

Salads

Chilled Pasta Salad

4 ounces linguine
1 cup thinly sliced fresh
    mushrooms
1 carrot, shredded (½ cup)
¼ cup sliced green onion
6 cherry tomatoes, halved
2 tablespoons salad oil
2 tablespoons soy sauce
2 tablespoons lemon juice
½ teaspoon sesame oil
1 small clove garlic, minced
    Few drops bottled hot pepper
    sauce
2 tablespoons sesame seed,
    toasted

Cook linguine according to package directions. Rinse with cold water; drain well. In bowl combine linguine, sliced mushrooms, shredded carrot, green onion, and halved cherry tomatoes.

For dressing, in a screw-top jar combine salad oil, soy sauce, lemon juice, sesame oil, minced garlic, and hot pepper sauce. Cover and shake well. Pour dressing over linguine mixture and toss to coat. Cover and refrigerate for 3 to 24 hours, stirring occasionally.

Before serving: Toss well; sprinkle with toasted sesame seed. Garnish with parsley, if desired. Makes 6 servings.

Chilled Pasta Salad
Vegetables in Aspic

Vegetables In Aspic

When using cooked or canned vegetables, drain before folding into gelatin —

1 envelope unflavored gelatin
1 12-ounce can (1½ cups)
    vegetable juice cocktail
2 teaspoons instant chicken
    bouillon granules
½ teaspoon dried tarragon,
    crushed
¼ cup cold water
1 hard-cooked egg, sliced
8 to 10 fresh *or* frozen
    asparagus spears, crisp-
    cooked, drained, cooled,
    and chopped
1½ cups desired vegetables★
2 tablespoons thinly sliced
    green onion

In saucepan soften gelatin in ½ *cup* of the vegetable juice. Add bouillon granules and tarragon; heat to dissolve gelatin and bouillon. Remove from heat; add remaining vegetable juice and the cold water. Chill about ½ *cup* of the mixture till partially set (consistency of unbeaten egg whites); pour into the bottoms of six ½-cup fluted molds. Place *one* of the hard-cooked egg slices in each mold, pressing down into gelatin. Cover molds; chill till almost firm. Meanwhile, chill the remaining gelatin till partially set. Fold asparagus, desired vegetables, and green onion into partially set gelatin; spoon mixture over egg slice in each mold. Cover and refrigerate for 6 to 24 hours.

Before serving: Unmold onto serving plate; garnish with mayonnaise, if desired. Serves 6.

★ **Vegetable options:** Choose one or any combination of the following: Finely shredded cabbage; sliced fresh mushrooms; uncooked pea pods; uncooked shelled peas; chopped, unpeeled cucumber or zucchini; cooked broccoli cuts; cooked cauliflower flowerets; cooked green or red pepper strips; cooked dry lentils; canned garbanzo beans; canned red kidney beans; canned lima beans; or canned navy beans.

Mushroom-Zucchini Salad

2½ cups sliced fresh mushrooms
1 medium zucchini *or*
    cucumber, thinly sliced
1 medium tomato, chopped
¼ cup sliced green onion
2 tablespoons salad oil
2 tablespoons vinegar
½ teaspoon salt
½ teaspoon dried marjoram,
    crushed
½ teaspoon pepper

In salad bowl combine mushrooms, zucchini or cucumber, tomato, and green onion.

For dressing, in a screw-top jar combine salad oil, vinegar, salt, marjoram, and pepper. Cover and shake well to mix; pour over vegetables. Toss to coat. Cover and refrigerate for 3 to 24 hours.

Before serving: Toss salad well. Makes 6 servings.

Salads

Cottage Potato Salad

    2 tablespoons all-purpose flour
    2 tablespoons sugar
 2½ teaspoons salt
      Dash ground red pepper
    ¾ cup milk
    2 slightly beaten egg yolks
    1 tablespoon prepared mustard
    ¼ cup vinegar
    2 teaspoons butter *or*
        margarine, melted
    4 cups diced cooked potatoes
    1 cup thinly sliced celery
    ½ cup chopped green pepper
    2 hard-cooked eggs, chopped
    2 tablespoons chopped onion
    1 cup cream-style cottage
        cheese with chives
      Lettuce cups

For dressing, in saucepan combine flour, sugar, salt, and red pepper. Stir in milk, egg yolks, and mustard. Cook and stir over low heat till thickened and bubbly. Cook and stir 1 to 2 minutes more. Add vinegar and melted butter or margarine; stir till well blended. Cool.

In large bowl stir together diced cooked potatoes, sliced celery, chopped green pepper, chopped eggs, and chopped onion. Combine cottage cheese and the cooked dressing. Pour cheese-dressing mixture over potato mixture. Toss to coat. Cover and refrigerate for 3 to 24 hours.

Before serving: Spoon potato salad into lettuce cups. Makes 8 to 10 servings.

Mint Tabouli Salad with Yogurt

This wholesome bulgur salad originated in Syria and Lebanon —

    2 cups hot water
    ¾ cup bulgur wheat
    1 cup fresh *or* frozen peas
    2 medium tomatoes, chopped
        (1½ cups)
    1 cup snipped parsley
    ½ cup roasted soybeans
    ¼ cup sliced green onion
    4 teaspoons snipped fresh mint
        or 1 teaspoon dried mint,
        crushed
    ½ teaspoon salt
    ⅛ teaspoon pepper
    ¼ cup lemon juice
    2 tablespoons cooking oil
    1 tablespoon olive oil *or*
        salad oil
      Lettuce leaves
    ½ cup plain yogurt

In mixing bowl combine the hot water and bulgur wheat. Let stand 1 hour. Drain. Thaw peas, if frozen. Combine bulgur, peas, chopped tomatoes, parsley, roasted soybeans, green onion, mint, salt, and pepper. Stir together lemon juice, cooking oil, and olive oil; pour over bulgur mixture. Toss well. Cover and refrigerate for 3 to 24 hours.

Before serving: Spoon salad mixture onto lettuce-lined plates. Top each serving with *2 tablespoons* of the plain yogurt. Makes 4 servings.

Spiced Peach Salad

    1 29-ounce can spiced whole
        peaches
    4 medium oranges
    1 6-ounce package lemon-
        flavored gelatin
    2 cups boiling water
    ½ cup chopped pecans
    1 4-ounce jar maraschino
        cherries, drained and
        halved (½ cup)
      Lettuce leaves

Drain peaches, reserving syrup. Pit and chop peaches. Peel and section oranges over bowl to catch juice. Combine the orange juice and reserved peach syrup; add cold *water,* if necessary, to make 2 cups liquid. Set aside. Dissolve gelatin in boiling water. Add reserved syrup mixture. Chill till partially set. Fold in chopped peaches, orange sections, pecans, and cherry halves. Turn into an 8-cup mold. Cover and refrigerate for 6 to 24 hours.

Before serving: Unmold gelatin salad onto lettuce-lined platter. Makes 10 servings.

Unmolding Salads

To unmold a gelatin salad, loosen edge (and around center of ring mold) with spatula. Dip mold in warm water for a *few seconds;* tilt slightly. Tilt and rotate mold so air can loosen gelatin all the way around. Place plate upside down over mold; hold plate and mold together. Invert; lift off mold.

Layered Cranberry-Apple Mold

Pictured on pages 60 and 61 —

    1 6-ounce package lemon-
         flavored gelatin
    ½ cup sugar
    1½ cups boiling water
    1½ cups cranberry-apple drink
    1 8-ounce can (¾ cup) whole
         cranberry sauce
    1 1½-ounce envelope dessert
         topping mix
    ⅓ cup mayonnaise *or* salad
         dressing
    1 large unpeeled apple, cored
         and finely chopped (1¼
         cups)
       Lettuce leaves
       Cranberries (optional)

Dissolve gelatin and sugar in boiling water. Add cranberry-apple drink. Chill 1¾ cups of mixture till partially set (consistency of unbeaten egg whites). Keep remaining mixture at room temperature.

Fold chilled gelatin mixture into cranberry sauce. Pour into a 7- to 8-cup ring mold; chill till *almost* firm. Chill remaining gelatin mixture till partially set.

Prepare topping mix according to package directions. Fold topping mix, mayonnaise, and apple into partially set gelatin mixture. Spoon apple mixture over gelatin layer in mold. Cover and refrigerate for 6 to 24 hours.

Before serving: Unmold onto lettuce-lined platter and garnish with fresh cranberries, if desired. Makes 12 servings.

Tangy Cabbage Slaw

    ⅓ cup sugar
    ⅓ cup vinegar
    ½ teaspoon salt
    ⅛ teaspoon pepper
    6 cups finely shredded
         cabbage (1¼ pounds)
    ¼ cup finely chopped onion
    ¼ cup chopped green pepper
    ¼ cup shredded carrot

For dressing, in saucepan heat sugar, vinegar, salt, and pepper, stirring constantly till sugar dissolves. Cool. In bowl combine cabbage, onion, green pepper, and carrot. Pour dressing over vegetable mixture; toss to coat. Cover and refrigerate for 3 to 24 hours. Makes 4 to 6 servings.

Cinnamon-Orange Rolls

Pictured on page 71 —

    4 to 4½ cups all-purpose flour
    1 package active dry yeast
    1 cup milk
    ⅓ cup packed brown sugar
    ⅓ cup butter *or* margarine
    1 tablespoon finely shredded
         orange peel
    1 teaspoon salt
    2 eggs
    3 tablespoons butter *or*
         margarine
    ⅔ cup packed brown sugar
    ½ cup chopped walnuts
    2 teaspoons ground cinnamon
    1½ cups sifted powdered sugar
    2 to 3 tablespoons orange juice

In mixer bowl combine *2 cups* flour and the yeast. In saucepan heat milk, the ⅓ cup brown sugar, the ⅓ cup butter or margarine, orange peel, and salt just till warm (115° to 120°) and butter is almost melted; stir constantly. Add to flour mixture; add eggs. Beat at low speed of electric mixer for ½ minute, scraping sides of bowl constantly. Beat 3 minutes at high speed. Stir in as much of the remaining flour as you can mix in with a spoon. Turn out onto lightly floured surface. Knead in enough of the remaining flour to make a moderately stiff dough that is smooth and elastic (6 to 8 minutes total). Cover; let rest 15 minutes. Punch down; divide dough in half.

Roll *one half* into a 12x8-inch rectangle. Melt the 3 tablespoons butter or margarine; brush *half* over dough. Combine the ⅔ cup brown sugar, chopped walnuts, and cinnamon; sprinkle *half* over dough. Roll up jelly-roll style, beginning with longest side. Pinch edges to seal seam. Cut into 1-inch slices. Place in greased 9x1½-inch round baking pan. Repeat with the remaining dough, butter, and sugar mixture. Cover with moisture-vaporproof wrap. Seal, label, and freeze.

Before serving: Thaw at room temperature for 2 hours or overnight in refrigerator. Uncover; let rise in warm place till double (1¾ to 2 hours). Bake in 375° oven for 20 to 25 minutes or till done. Cool slightly; invert onto wire rack to cool. Invert onto serving plate. Meanwhile, combine powdered sugar and enough orange juice to make of drizzling consistency. Drizzle over rolls. Makes 24 rolls.

Breads

Brown-and-Serve Rolls

3½ to 4 cups all-purpose flour
1 package active dry yeast
1½ cups milk
¼ cup sugar
¼ cup shortening
1 egg

In large mixer bowl combine *2 cups* of the flour and the yeast. In saucepan heat milk, sugar, shortening, and 1 teaspoon *salt* just till warm (115° to 120°) and shortening is almost melted; stir constantly. Add to flour mixture; add egg. Beat at low speed of electric mixer for ½ minute, scraping sides of bowl. Beat 3 minutes at high speed. Stir in as much of remaining flour as you can with a spoon. Turn out onto lightly floured surface. Knead in enough of the remaining flour to make a moderately stiff dough that is smooth and elastic (6 to 8 minutes total). Shape into ball.

Place in lightly greased bowl; turn once to grease surface. Cover; let rise in warm place till double (1½ to 2 hours). Punch down. Cover, let rest 10 minutes. Turn out onto floured surface; shape into desired roll shapes. Place on greased baking sheet or in greased muffin pans. Cover; let rise till double (about 45 minutes). Bake in 325° oven for 12 to 15 minutes; *do not brown.* Remove from pan; cool. Wrap in moisture-vaporproof wrap. Seal, label, and freeze.

Before serving: Thaw wrapped rolls at room temperature for 10 to 15 minutes. Unwrap; place on baking sheet. Bake in 400° oven for 5 to 10 minutes or till golden brown. Makes 24 to 36 rolls.

Freezer Whole Wheat Bread

3 cups whole wheat flour
1½ to 2 cups all-purpose flour
2 packages active dry yeast
⅓ cup nonfat dry milk powder
¼ cup sugar
2 tablespoons butter *or* margarine
½ cup toasted wheat germ
½ cup chopped nuts
Toasted wheat germ
Cooking oil

Combine *2 cups* of the whole wheat flour, *1 cup* of the all-purpose flour, the yeast, and milk powder.

Heat sugar, butter or margarine, 2 cups *water,* and 1 tablespoon *salt* just till warm (115° to 120°) and butter is almost melted; stir constantly. Add to flour mixture. Beat at low speed of electric mixer for ½ minute, scraping sides of bowl. Beat 3 minutes at high speed. Stir in ½ cup wheat germ and nuts. Stir in the remaining whole wheat flour and as much of remaining all-purpose flour as you can mix in with a spoon.

Turn out onto lightly floured surface. Knead in enough of the remaining all-purpose flour to make a stiff dough that is smooth and elastic (8 to 10 minutes). Cover; let rest 15 minutes. Punch down; divide dough in half. Shape dough into loaves. Roll in additional wheat germ. Wrap in plastic wrap; place in two 8x4x2-inch loaf pans. Freeze till firm. Remove from pans; overwrap in moisture-vaporproof wrap. Seal, label, and freeze.

Before serving: Remove wrap. Place in greased 8x4x2-inch loaf pan. Cover and thaw. Brush with oil. Cover; let rise till nearly double (1¼ to 1½ hours).

Bake in a 375° oven for 35 to 40 minutes or till bread tests done. Remove from pan; cool on wire rack. Makes 2 loaves.

Whole Wheat Nut Bread

1 cup all-purpose flour
1 cup whole wheat flour
½ cup packed brown sugar
¼ cup sugar
½ teaspoon baking soda
1 beaten egg
1 6-ounce can apricot nectar
1 teaspoon finely shredded lemon peel
2 tablespoons lemon juice
2 tablespoons cooking oil
½ cup coarsely chopped nuts

Stir together all-purpose flour, whole wheat flour, brown sugar, sugar, soda, and ½ teaspoon *salt.* Combine egg, nectar, lemon peel, lemon juice, and oil; add to dry ingredients, stirring just till moistened. Fold in nuts.

Turn into a greased 8x4x2-inch loaf pan. Bake in a 350° oven for 50 to 60 minutes or till done. Cool 10 minutes. Remove to wire rack; cool. Wrap in foil; store overnight before slicing.

Cinnamon-Orange Rolls (see recipe, page 69)
Freezer Whole Wheat Bread
Brown-and-Serve Rolls

Breads

Cornmeal Waffles

1 cup all-purpose flour
2 teaspoons baking powder
1 teaspoon baking soda
1 teaspoon sugar
½ teaspoon salt
1 cup yellow cornmeal
2 beaten egg yolks
2 cups buttermilk *or* sour milk
¼ cup cooking oil
2 stiff-beaten egg whites
   Butter *or* margarine (optional)
   Pancake and waffle syrup
   (optional)

In mixing bowl stir together flour, baking powder, baking soda, sugar, and salt. Stir in cornmeal. Combine egg yolks, buttermilk or sour milk, and cooking oil. Add to flour-cornmeal mixture all at once. Stir mixture till blended but still lumpy.

Carefully fold in beaten egg whites, leaving a few fluffs of egg white in batter. *Do not overmix.* Pour some batter onto grids of pre-heated lightly greased waffle baker. Close lid quickly; do not open during baking. Remove baked waffle from grid with a fork. Repeat with remaining batter till all is used. Cool. Place waffles on baking sheet; freeze firm. Wrap in moisture-vaporproof wrap. Seal, label, and freeze.

Before serving: Toast waffles. If desired, serve them with butter or margarine and pancake and waffle syrup. Makes four or five 9-inch waffles.

Raisin-Molasses Muffins

⅔ cup shortening
½ cup sugar
2 eggs
½ cup buttermilk *or* sour milk
½ cup molasses
2 cups all-purpose flour
2 teaspoons baking powder
½ teaspoon salt
½ teaspoon ground cinnamon
¼ teaspoon baking soda
¼ teaspoon ground cloves
⅛ teaspoon ground nutmeg
1 cup raisins

In mixer bowl beat shortening and sugar till fluffy. Add eggs, buttermilk or sour milk, and molasses; beat till well combined. Stir together the flour, baking powder, salt, cinnamon, baking soda, cloves, and nutmeg; stir into beaten mixture. Fold in raisins. Turn batter into an airtight container. Cover and store in refrigerator up to 10 days.

Before serving: Without stirring batter, fill greased or paper bake cup-lined muffin pans ⅔ full. Bake in 350° oven for 25 to 30 minutes or till golden. Makes 18 to 20 muffins.

● **Microwave directions:** Prepare and store muffin batter as directed above. Before serving, without stirring batter, fill greased or paper bake cup-lined nonmetal muffin pans ⅔ full. Cook 6 muffins at a time in counter-top microwave oven on high power for 2 to 2¼ minutes or till done.

Pecan Pizza Coffee Cake

½ cup whole bran cereal,
   coarsely crushed
¼ cup sugar
1 package active dry yeast
½ cup warm water (110° to
   115°)
1 egg
1½ cups all-purpose flour
1 tablespoon cooking oil
1 cup chopped pecans
⅓ cup packed brown sugar
¼ cup maple-flavored syrup
2 tablespoons butter *or*
   margarine
1 teaspoon ground cinnamon

Combine cereal, sugar, and yeast. Stir in water. Let stand 5 minutes. Add egg, ½ *cup* of the flour, the oil, and ½ teaspoon *salt*. Beat at low speed of electric mixter for ½ minute or till blended. Beat at high speed 3 minutes, scraping bowl. By hand, stir in remaining flour. Knead 1 minute. Place in greased bowl. Cover; let rise till double (about 1 hour). In saucepan combine pecans, brown sugar, syrup, butter or margarine, and cinnamon. Cook and stir over low heat just till sugar dissolves. *Do not boil.* Set aside. Punch dough down. Cover, let rest 10 minutes. With floured hands press dough into a greased 12-inch round pizza pan or two greased 9x1½-inch round baking pans, forming a high edge. Crimp edge; spread pecan mixture to within 1 inch of edge. Bake in 400° oven about 20 minutes. (If using a 12-inch pizza pan, place on a baking sheet to bake.) Cool. Cover, seal, label, and freeze.

Before serving: Thaw at room temperature. Makes 1 or 2.

Rice and Pasta

Chilled Rice and Pea Pods

You can store tightly covered or wrapped cooked rice for up to 1 week in the refrigerator or up to 6 months in the freezer —

1½ cups cooked rice, chilled
⅓ cup chopped celery
6 radishes, thinly sliced (⅓ cup)
2 tablespoons sliced green onion
2 tablespoons snipped parsley
2 tablespoons water
2 tablespoons salad oil
2 tablespoons lemon juice
1 teaspoon sugar
¾ teaspoon dried basil, crushed
½ teaspoon salt
　Dash pepper
1 6-ounce package frozen pea pods, thawed
　Parsley sprigs (optional)

In bowl combine rice, celery, radishes, green onion, and parsley. Toss to mix.

In screw-top jar combine water, salad oil, lemon juice, sugar, basil, salt, and pepper. Shake to mix well; pour over rice mixture. Toss to coat. Cover and refrigerate for 3 to 24 hours.

Before serving: Add pea pods to rice mixture; toss to mix. Garnish with parsley sprigs, if desired. Makes 4 to 6 servings.

Fruited Oven Rice

2 cups boiling water
2 tablespoons butter *or* margarine
2 teaspoons instant chicken bouillon granules
1 cup long grain rice
3 tablespoons finely snipped dried apricots
1 teaspoon finely shredded lemon peel
¼ teaspoon salt
⅓ cup raisins
　Sliced almonds

In a 1-quart casserole combine the boiling water, butter or margarine, and chicken bouillon granules, stirring till the butter melts. Stir in the uncooked rice, snipped dried apricots, shredded lemon peel, and salt. Cover and refrigerate for 3 to 24 hours.

Before serving: Bake casserole, covered, in a 350° oven about 30 minutes. Stir in the raisins. Sprinkle with almonds. Bake, covered, 35 minutes more or till rice is tender. Makes 4 servings.

Homemade Parsley Noodles

1 cup lightly packed fresh parsley sprigs (stems removed)
1 egg
2 tablespoons milk
½ teaspoon salt
1 cup all-purpose flour

Rinse and drain parsley sprigs. In blender container or food processor bowl combine parsley, egg, milk, and salt. Cover and blend mixture till smooth. Transfer mixture to a mixing bowl. Stir in the flour till mixture forms a ball.

On lightly floured surface roll the dough to a 16x12-inch rectangle. Let stand 20 minutes. Roll up dough loosely. Cut dough crosswise into ¼-inch-thick slices; unroll. Cut noodles into desired lengths. Spread out noodles on wire racks and let stand, uncovered, at room temperature about 2 hours to dry. Cover and store in refrigerator.

Before serving: Drop the dried noodles into a large amount of boiling salted water, broth, or soup. Cook, uncovered, for 10 to 12 minutes or till done. Makes 6 ounces (2½ cups cooked noodles).

Storing Cooked Pasta

To store cooked pasta, cook according to package directions; drain well. Stir in a small amount of cooking oil. Place the pasta in an airtight container. Cover and refrigerate for as long as 1 week. Before serving, dip the chilled cooked pasta in hot water to reheat.

Desserts

Cakes, cookies, pies, and parfaits are just a sampling of the choice desserts you'll find in this chapter.

Prepare one of these tempting creations at your leisure so it's ready to serve unexpected guests. Or, you might like to make a dessert in advance to highlight a family meal later in the week.

Whatever the occasion, there's a make-ahead dessert that is appropriate. You'll find cakes and ice cream desserts that freeze, mousse and cheesecake that wait in the refrigerator, and other desserts that can be kept at room temperature.

No matter which make-ahead recipe you choose, last-minute preparation has been streamlined or eliminated so that your final tasks will be as easy as possible.

Blueberry and Sour Cream Torte (see recipe, page 79)
Ready-to-Bake Chocolate Chippers (see recipe, page 78)
Whole Wheat Carrot Cake (see recipe, page 77)
Raspberry Bavarian (see recipe, page 82)

Pineapple Cake Roll

1 15½-ounce can crushed
   pineapple
½ cup packed brown sugar
2 tablespoons butter *or*
   margarine, melted
½ cup all-purpose flour
1 teaspoon baking powder
¼ teaspoon salt
4 egg yolks
½ teaspoon vanilla
⅓ cup sugar
4 egg whites
½ cup sugar
   Sifted powdered sugar
   Pineapple Sauce

Drain pineapple, reserving syrup. If necessary, add water to syrup to make ¾ cup liquid; set aside for sauce.

Stir together the drained pineapple, brown sugar, and melted butter or margarine; spread mixture evenly in bottom of ungreased 15x10x1-inch jelly roll pan. Stir together flour, baking powder, and salt. In small mixer bowl beat egg yolks and vanilla about 5 minutes or till thick and lemon-colored. Gradually add the ⅓ cup sugar, beating till sugar dissolves. Thoroughly wash beaters.

Beat egg whites to soft peaks. Gradually add the ½ cup sugar, beating to stiff peaks. Fold yolk mixture into whites. Sprinkle flour mixture over egg mixture. Fold in lightly by hand. Spread batter over pineapple mixture in pan. Bake in 375° oven for 12 to 15 minutes. Immediately loosen edges of cake from pan and turn out onto towel sprinkled with powdered sugar. (If any pineapple mixture remains in pan, remove with narrow spat-ula and spread over cake.) Let stand 1 minute. Starting with narrow end, roll up cake, using towel to help you roll. Cool completely on wire rack. Place on serving plate. Cover and refrigerate for 3 to 24 hours. Prepare Pineapple Sauce.

Before serving: Cut into ½-inch slices; place 2 slices on each plate. Spoon Pineapple Sauce over. Makes 10 servings.

Pineapple Sauce: In medium saucepan stir together ¼ cup *sugar* and 1 tablespoon *cornstarch.* Add reserved pineapple syrup. Cook and stir till bubbly; continue 2 minutes more. Stir in 1 tablespoon *butter* and a few drops of *yellow food coloring,* if desired. Cover surface with waxed paper; chill.

Nutmeg Torte

Pictured on page 81 —

½ cup butter *or* margarine
3 eggs
1½ cups all-purpose flour
¾ teaspoon ground nutmeg
½ teaspoon baking powder
¼ teaspoon salt
1⅓ cups sugar
1 teaspoon vanilla
½ cup dairy sour cream
2 3-ounce packages cream
   cheese
½ cup butter *or* margarine
2 teaspoons vanilla
4 cups sifted powdered sugar
1 to 2 tablespoons milk
1 cup chopped walnuts
   Apricot preserves
   Candied violets (optional)

Bring ½ cup butter or margarine and eggs to room temperature. Grease two 7x3½x2-inch loaf pans. Stir together flour, nutmeg, baking powder, and salt. In mixer bowl beat ½ cup butter with electric mixer till fluffy. Gradually add sugar, beating till fluffy. Add eggs, one at a time, beating 1 minute after each; scrape bowl frequently, guiding mixture toward beaters. Add 1 teaspoon vanilla; beat well.

Add dry ingredients and sour cream alternately to beaten mixture, beating after each addition just till combined. Turn batter into prepared pans. Bake in a 325° oven for 55 to 60 minutes or till cakes test done. Cool 10 minutes on wire racks. Remove from pans; cool. Slice each cake horizontally into 3 layers.

Meanwhile, beat together cream cheese, ½ cup butter or margarine, and 2 teaspoons vanilla till light and fluffy. Gradually add powdered sugar, beating till smooth. Beat in enough milk to make fluffy consistency. Set aside ½ cup cream cheese mixture. To remaining mixture fold in nuts. Spread the bottom cake layers with *half* of the nut filling. Top with next layers and remaining nut filling. Top with final cake layers. Spread tops with apricot preserves. Dollop or pipe on reserved frosting.

Freeze till firm; wrap with moisture-vaporproof wrap. Seal, label, and freeze.

Before serving: Thaw cakes at room temperature about 2 hours. Garnish with candied violets, if desired. Makes 2 cakes, 8 servings each.

Whole Wheat Carrot Cake

Pictured on pages 74 and 75 —

2 cups whole wheat flour
⅓ cup nonfat dry milk powder
2 teaspoons ground cinnamon
1 teaspoon baking soda
1 teaspoon baking powder
1 cup cooking oil
1 cup sugar
1 cup packed brown sugar
1 teaspoon vanilla
4 eggs
3 cups finely shredded carrots
¾ cup chopped walnuts
¼ cup toasted wheat germ
⅓ cup packed brown sugar
2 tablespoons butter *or* margarine, melted

Grease and lightly flour two 8x8x2-inch or two 9x1½-inch round baking pans. Set aside. Stir together flour, dry milk powder, cinnamon, baking soda, baking powder, and 1 teaspoon *salt*. In large mixer bowl beat oil, sugar, and 1 cup brown sugar on low speed of electric mixer till mixed. Beat in vanilla. Add eggs, one at a time, beating well after each addition. Add dry ingredients to egg mixture, beating till well combined. By hand, stir in carrots. Pour batter into pans.

Combine nuts, wheat germ, ⅓ cup brown sugar, and melted butter. Top batter evenly with nut mixture. Bake in 350° oven for 30 to 35 minutes or till cakes test done. Cool in pans on wire racks. Cover with moisture-vaporproof wrap. Seal, label, and freeze.

Before serving: Thaw at room temperature about 1 hour. Cut into squares or wedges. Serves 12.

Date-Pecan Cupcakes

1 8-ounce package (1⅓ cups) pitted whole dates, snipped
1⅓ cups boiling water
2¼ cups all-purpose flour
1 teaspoon baking soda
1 teaspoon salt
1⅓ cups sugar
¾ cup shortening
2 eggs
½ cup chopped pecans
   Sifted powdered sugar

In small bowl combine dates and boiling water; cool to room temperature. Stir together flour, baking soda, and salt. In mixer bowl beat shortening on medium speed of electric mixer about 30 seconds. Add sugar and beat till fluffy. Add eggs, one at a time, beating 1 minute after each.

Add dry ingredients and date mixture alternately to beaten mixture, beating on low speed after each addition just till combined. Stir in chopped nuts. Fill paper bake cups in muffin pans ½ full with cake batter. Bake in 375° oven for 18 to 20 minutes or till done. Cool on wire rack. Sprinkle with sifted powdered sugar. Place in plastic freezer bags. Seal, label, and freeze.

Before serving: Thaw cupcakes at room temperature. Makes about 30 cupcakes.

Almond Fruitcake

1½ cups butter *or* margarine
1 cup sugar
6 eggs
2 tablespoons brandy
1 teaspoon finely shredded lemon peel
4 cups all-purpose flour
1½ cups diced mixed candied fruits and peels (12 ounces)
1 cup dried currants
1 8-ounce can almond paste
   Brandy

Grease two 8x4x2-inch loaf pans. In large mixer bowl beat butter or margarine on medium speed of electric mixer about 30 seconds. Add sugar and beat till fluffy. Add eggs, one at a time, beating 1 minute after each. Stir in 2 tablespoons brandy and the lemon peel. Stir in flour, fruits and peels, and currants. Spread 1¼ *cups* of the batter into *each* of the prepared pans. Divide almond paste into fourths. On floured surface roll each portion of almond paste to an 8x4-inch rectangle. Place one rectangle over batter in each pan; top *each* with 1¼ *cups* batter, a second almond rectangle, and *half* the remaining batter. Bake in 350° oven for 50 to 60 minutes or till done. Cool in pans on wire racks; remove from pans. Wrap cakes in brandy-soaked cloth, then in foil. Store cakes in refrigerator at least 1 week. Remoisten cloth as needed.

Before serving: Unwrap loaf; slice. Makes 2 loaves.

Desserts

Chocolate Pie Cookies

2 cups all-purpose flour
⅔ cup unsweetened cocoa
    powder
1 teaspoon baking soda
½ cup shortening
1 cup sugar
1 egg
1 egg yolk
⅔ cup buttermilk
½ cup water
2 cups sifted powdered sugar
1 egg white
1 teaspoon vanilla
½ cup shortening
¼ cup butter *or* margarine,
    softened

Stir together the flour, cocoa powder, baking soda, and ¼ teaspoon *salt*. In mixer bowl beat ½ cup shortening for 30 seconds. Add sugar and beat till fluffy. Add the egg and egg yolk; beat well. Add dry ingredients, buttermilk, and water alternately to beaten mixture and beat till well blended. Drop batter by rounded tablespoonfuls 2 inches apart onto an ungreased cookie sheet. Bake in a 350° oven for 8 to 10 minutes. Remove to wire rack; cool.

Meanwhile, to make filling, in mixer bowl combine powdered sugar, egg white, and vanilla. Beat on low speed of electric mixer, gradually adding the ½ cup shortening and the butter or margarine. Beat at high speed till light and fluffy. Spread some filling on the bottom side of one cookie; top with second cookie to form sandwich. Repeat with remaining cookies. Cover and store in refrigerator. Makes about 24 filled cookies.

Ready-to-Bake Chocolate Chippers

Pictured on pages 74 and 75 —

¾ cup all-purpose flour
¾ cup whole wheat flour
1 teaspoon baking soda
½ cup butter *or* margarine
½ cup shortening
1 cup sugar
1 cup packed brown sugar
2 eggs
1 teaspoon vanilla
3 cups quick-cooking rolled
    oats
1 6-ounce package (1 cup)
    semisweet chocolate
    pieces

Mix first 3 ingredients. Beat butter and shortening 30 seconds. Add sugars; beat till fluffy. Beat in eggs and vanilla. Beat in dry ingredients. Stir in oats and chocolate. Shape into 1-inch balls. Flatten and freeze on cookie sheets. Place in freezer bags. Seal, label, and freeze.

Before serving: Place frozen dough on ungreased cookie sheet. Bake in a 375° oven 12 minutes. Remove to rack; cool. Makes 72.

Sunflower and Oat Cookies

1½ cups quick-cooking rolled
    oats
1 cup whole wheat flour
½ teaspoon baking soda
½ cup butter *or* margarine
½ cup sugar
½ cup packed brown sugar
1 egg

2 tablespoons milk
½ teaspoon vanilla
½ cup sunflower nuts

Combine the oats, flour, baking soda, and ¼ teaspoon *salt*. Beat butter 30 seconds. Add sugars; beat till fluffy. Add egg, milk, and vanilla; beat well. Stir in dry ingredients. Stir in sunflower nuts. Drop dough from a teaspoon onto ungreased cookie sheet. Bake in 350° oven 10 to 12 minutes. Cool 1 minute; remove to wire rack. Cool. Place in freezer container. Cover, seal, label, and freeze.

Before serving: Thaw at room temperature. Makes 36 cookies.

Chilled Pecan-Lime Pie

1 3-ounce package lime-
    flavored gelatin
1 teaspoon finely shredded
    lime peel
¼ cup lime juice
1 cup evaporated milk
½ cup chopped pecans
1 4½-ounce container frozen
    whipped dessert topping,
    thawed
1 purchased chocolate-flavored
    crumb pie shell
Lime twists (optional)

Dissolve gelatin in ½ cup *boiling water*. Stir in lime peel and juice. Stir in evaporated milk. Chill till partially set. Stir in the nuts. Fold thawed dessert topping into mixture. Chill till mixture mounds when spooned. Turn into pie shell. Refrigerate for 3 to 24 hours.

Before serving: Garnish with lime twists, if desired.

Date-Nut Ice Cream Pie

1 stick piecrust mix
1 quart vanilla ice cream
⅔ cup pitted whole dates,
    snipped (4 ounces)
⅓ cup water
2 teaspoons sugar
1 tablespoon lemon juice
½ teaspoon vanilla
2 tablespoons chopped walnuts
½ of a 4½-ounce carton (1 cup)
    frozen whipped dessert
    topping, thawed
    Walnut halves

Prepare piecrust mix according to package directions, fitting it into a 9-inch pie plate. Flute edges and prick pastry. Bake in 450° oven for 10 to 12 minutes or till golden. Cool.

In mixing bowl soften ice cream using wooden spoon to stir and press against side of bowl. Soften just till pliable. Using a metal spatula, spread ice cream into bottom of cooled pastry shell. Freeze till firm.

Meanwhile, in saucepan combine snipped dates, water, and sugar. Bring to boiling. Simmer, covered, about 5 minutes or till dates are softened. Stir in the lemon juice and vanilla; cool.

Spread ½ *cup* of the date mixture over frozen ice cream layer in pastry shell. Fold remaining date mixture and the chopped walnuts into thawed whipped topping. Spread over date layer. Freeze till firm. Cover with moisture-vapor-proof wrap. Seal, label, and freeze.

Before serving: Let pie stand at room temperature 10 to 15 minutes. Garnish with walnut halves. Slice pie and serve immediately.

Sweet Potato Cheesecake

2½ cups finely crushed vanilla
    wafers (about 55 cookies)
½ cup butter *or* margarine,
    melted
2 medium sweet potatoes,
    cooked, peeled, and
    cooled
2 8-ounce packages cream
    cheese, softened
⅔ cup sugar
2 eggs
2 cups dairy sour cream
¼ cup orange liqueur
1 teaspoon ground cinnamon
    Orange slices (optional)

In medium bowl combine crushed wafers and butter or margarine. Press mixture firmly over bottom and 2 inches up sides of 9-inch springform pan. Chill 1 hour. Place cooked sweet potatoes in blender container or food processor bowl; puree (to make about 1 cup) and set aside. In mixer bowl beat together cream cheese and sugar on medium speed of electric mixer till fluffy. Beat in eggs just till combined. Stir in pureed sweet potatoes, the sour cream, orange liqueur, and cinnamon. Pour into prepared crust. Bake in a 350° oven for 55 to 60 minutes or till cheesecake is set. Cool in pan on wire rack. Refrigerate for 3 to 24 hours.

Before serving: Loosen sides and remove rim of pan. Place on serving plate. Garnish with orange slices, if desired. Serves 10 to 12.

Blueberry and Sour Cream Torte

Pictured on pages 74 and 75 —

¾ cup butter *or* margarine
¼ cup sugar
2 egg yolks
2 cups all-purpose flour
1 teaspoon baking powder
4 cups fresh blueberries
½ cup sugar
¼ cup quick-cooking tapioca
½ teaspoon finely shredded
    lemon peel
½ teaspoon ground cinnamon
⅛ teaspoon ground nutmeg
2 slightly beaten egg yolks
2 cups dairy sour cream
½ cup sugar
1 teaspoon vanilla

Beat together butter and ¼ cup sugar. Add 2 egg yolks; beat till fluffy. Combine flour, baking powder, and ½ teaspoon *salt*. Stir into beaten mixture. Press *two-thirds* of the mixture onto the bottom of a 9-inch springform pan. Bake in 400° oven 10 minutes. Cool. Reduce oven temperature to 350°. Press remaining mixture 1½ inches up sides of pan. Combine berries, ½ cup sugar, tapioca, lemon peel, cinnamon, and nutmeg; let stand 15 minutes. Cook and stir till bubbly. Turn into crust.

For topper, beat together 2 egg yolks, sour cream, ½ cup sugar, and vanilla. Spoon over berry layer. Bake in 350° oven 45 minutes. Cool. Refrigerate 3 to 24 hours.

Before serving: Loosen sides and remove rim of pan. Place on serving plate. Garnish with finely shredded orange peel, if desired. Makes 10 to 12 servings.

Chocolate Mousse En Phyllo

6 18x12-inch sheets phyllo
   dough
6 tablespoons butter *or*
   margarine, melted
5 egg whites
1 envelope unflavored gelatin
1 6-ounce package (1 cup)
   semisweet chocolate
   pieces
½ cup butter *or* margarine
1 teaspoon instant coffee
   crystals
4 egg yolks
¼ cup brandy
½ cup sugar
1 tablespoon sugar

Generously grease a 9-inch springform pan with removable bottom. Stack phyllo dough sheets in bottom and up sides of pan, brushing each with some of the melted butter and letting sheets overlap pan edges. Trim dough to pan edge; crumble trimmings into pan. Brush trimmings with remaining melted butter. Bake in 375° oven about 20 minutes or till puffed and golden (crust will flatten on cooling). Combine *one* egg white and 1 tablespoon *water;* immediately brush over hot crust. Cool.

Soften gelatin in ⅓ cup *cold water.* Heat and stir till gelatin is dissolved. Stir in chocolate pieces, ½ cup butter, and the coffee crystals; heat and stir till melted. Remove from heat; set aside. In top of double boiler combine the egg yolks and brandy; beat till frothy. Gradually beat in the ½ cup sugar till yolks are thick and lemon-colored. Place over simmering water (upper pan should not touch water). Cook

and stir about 8 minutes or just till slightly thicker. *Do not overcook.* Place pan over cold water; beat 3 to 4 minutes or till consistency of mayonnaise. Stir chocolate mixture into yolk mixture. Wash beaters well. Beat remaining egg whites to soft peaks (tips curl over); gradually add the 1 tablespoon sugar, beating to stiff peaks. Fold chocolate mixture into egg white mixture. Pour into baked crust. Cover and refrigerate for 3 to 24 hours.

Before serving: Remove from pan; top with whipped cream and sliced toasted almonds, if desired. Cut into thin wedges. Serves 12.

Apricot Mousse

1 8¾-ounce can unpeeled
   apricot halves
¼ cup sugar
1 envelope unflavored gelatin
1 12-ounce can apricot nectar
1 cup whipping cream

Drain apricots, reserving ¼ cup syrup. Finely chop fruit. In saucepan combine sugar and gelatin. Add about *half* of the apricot nectar. Heat and stir till gelatin is dissolved. Remove from heat; stir in remaining nectar and reserved syrup. Chill till partially set (consistency of unbeaten egg whites).

Whip cream to soft peaks; fold into partially set gelatin. Fold in chopped apricots. Turn into serving bowl. (If desired, turn into 3-cup soufflé dish with collar. Remove collar before serving.) Refrigerate for 3 to 24 hours before serving. Makes 6 to 8 servings.

Fresh Fruit Trifle

2 cups desired fresh fruits★
8 cups sponge cake cut into
   ½-inch cubes
¼ cup cream sherry
½ cup desired jam *or* preserves
2 eggs
1 egg yolk
1¾ cups light cream
¼ cup sugar
1 egg white
1 tablespoon powdered sugar
½ cup whipping cream
¼ teaspoon vanilla

If necessary, brush fruits with lemon juice to prevent browning. Place *half* the cake in a 2- to 2½-quart bowl; sprinkle *half* the sherry over. Dot with jam. Layer fruit atop. Top with remaining cake. Sprinkle with remaining sherry.

For custard, beat eggs and yolk. Add cream and sugar. Cook and stir till custard coats a spoon. Place pan in ice water; cool, stirring occasionally. Spoon over cake.

Beat egg white to soft peaks. Gradually add powdered sugar, beating to stiff peaks. Whip cream with vanilla. Fold into egg white; spoon atop custard. Cover; refrigerate for 6 to 24 hours.

Before serving: Garnish with milk chocolate squares, if desired. Serves 10 to 12.

★ **Fruit options:** Choose combination of the following: sliced apricots, bananas, nectarines, peaches, pears, *or* strawberries; cubed mango, papaya, *or* pineapple.

Nutmeg Torte (see recipe, page 76)
Fresh Fruit Trifle

Caramel Charlotte Russe

9 ladyfingers, split
1 envelope unflavored gelatin
¼ cup cold water
1 cup sugar
½ cup boiling water
1 cup whipping cream
1 teaspoon vanilla
3 egg whites
¼ teaspoon cream of tartar
½ cup sliced almonds, toasted
   Mandarin orange sections
      (optional)
   Whipped cream (optional)

Place ladyfingers, uncut side out, around sides of a 1½-quart bowl or casserole, cutting ladyfingers as necessary to fit; set aside. Soften gelatin in cold water. Place sugar in heavy skillet; heat and stir over medium-low heat till sugar melts and turns golden brown. Remove from heat. Add boiling water *very slowly*, stirring constantly. Return to heat. Add softened gelatin; heat and stir till dissolved. Chill till the consistency of corn syrup, stirring occasionally. Remove from refrigerator; let stand while beating the whipping cream and egg whites.

Beat the 1 cup whipping cream and vanilla to soft peaks; refrigerate. Wash beaters thoroughly. Immediately beat egg whites and cream of tartar till stiff peaks form (tips stand straight). When gelatin is partially set (the consistency of unbeaten egg whites), fold gelatin mixture into stiff-beaten egg whites. Fold in whipped cream and almonds. Turn into ladyfinger-lined bowl. Refrigerate for 3 to 24 hours.

Before serving: Unmold onto serving plate. Garnish with mandarin orange sections and additional whipped cream, if desired. Makes 8 servings.

Baked Apple-Rice Pudding

2 slightly beaten egg yolks
2 medium apples, peeled, cored, and finely chopped (2 cups)
1½ cups cooked rice
½ cup milk
½ cup pitted whole dates, snipped
¼ cup sugar
2 tablespoons butter *or* margarine, melted
1 teaspoon vanilla
2 egg whites
   Apple slices (optional)

In bowl stir together egg yolks, chopped apples, cooked rice, milk, snipped dates, sugar, butter or margarine, and vanilla. Beat egg whites till stiff peaks form (tips stand straight). Fold egg whites into apple mixture. Turn into a 1½-quart baking dish or soufflé dish. Place in a larger baking pan. Set on oven rack. Pour boiling water into larger pan to a depth of 1 inch. Bake in 325° oven for 70 to 75 minutes. Refrigerate for 3 to 24 hours or serve warm.

Before serving: Garnish with fresh apple slices dipped in lemon juice, if desired. Makes 6 servings.

Raspberry Bavarian

Pictured on pages 74 and 75 —

1 envelope unflavored gelatin
½ cup raspberry-flavored pancake syrup
½ cup milk
2 slightly beaten egg yolks
   Few drops red food coloring (optional)
1 cup whipping cream
2 stiff-beaten egg whites
1 10-ounce package frozen red raspberries, thawed
2 tablespoons sugar
2 teaspoons cornstarch

In a 1½-quart saucepan soften gelatin in ¼ cup *water*. Stir in the pancake syrup, milk, and egg yolks. Cook and stir over low heat about 5 minutes or till gelatin is dissolved and mixture just bubbles. Stir in red food coloring, if desired. Set pan in bowl of ice. Chill till partially set (consistency of unbeaten egg whites), stirring frequently. (Do not allow to become too set.)

Meanwhile, whip cream to soft peaks. Fold egg whites into gelatin mixture; fold in whipped cream. Turn mixture into a 4-cup mold. Refrigerate 6 to 24 hours.

For raspberry sauce, drain raspberries, reserving ¼ cup syrup. In a small saucepan combine sugar and cornstarch; stir in the reserved syrup. Cook and stir till thickened and bubbly. Continue 2 minutes more. Cool slightly; stir in raspberries. Chill.

Before serving: Unmold Bavarian onto serving platter; spoon raspberry sauce atop. Serves 8.

Black Forest Squares

1 package 1-layer-size chocolate cake mix
1 cup dairy sour cream
1 package 4-serving-size *instant* chocolate pudding mix
1 cup milk
¼ cup crème de cassis *or* brandy
1 16-ounce can pitted dark sweet cherries
2 tablespoons sugar
1 tablespoon cornstarch
  Pressurized dessert topping
¼ cup sliced almonds, toasted

Grease and flour a 13x9x2-inch baking pan. Prepare cake mix according to package directions. Turn batter into prepared pan. Bake in a 350° oven for 10 to 12 minutes or till done. Cool in pan on wire rack.

In large mixer bowl beat together sour cream, dry pudding mix, ⅓ *cup* of the milk, and the crème de cassis or brandy till mixture is fluffy. Gradually add remaining milk, beating till smooth. Pour over chocolate cake. Cover and chill.

Meanwhile, drain cherries, reserving ¾ cup syrup. In a saucepan combine sugar and cornstarch. Gradually stir in the reserved syrup. Cook and stir over medium heat till thickened and bubbly. Cook and stir 2 minutes more. Add drained cherries. Cool. Spread over chilled layers. Cover and refrigerate for 3 to 24 hours.

Before serving: Pipe on dessert topping in a lattice design. Sprinkle with nuts. Cut into squares to serve. Makes 12 servings.

Apple-Chocolate Chip Bake

1 cup all-purpose flour
¼ cup packed brown sugar
6 tablespoons butter
1 21-ounce can apple pie filling
⅓ cup semisweet chocolate pieces
1 teaspoon ground cinnamon
¼ teaspoon ground cloves
1 cup dairy sour cream
1 slightly beaten egg
1 tablespoon sugar
1 teaspoon vanilla

Combine flour and brown sugar. Cut in butter till mixture resembles coarse crumbs. Press into an 8x8x2-inch baking dish. Bake in 400° oven 8 to 10 minutes. Cool. Combine pie filling, chocolate pieces, cinnamon, and cloves. Spread over cooled crust. Cover, seal, label, and freeze.

Before serving: Bake, uncovered, in 400° oven 35 minutes. Combine sour cream, egg, sugar, and vanilla; carefully spread over apple layer. Return to oven; bake 8 to 10 minutes more. Cool slightly; serve warm. Serves 12.

Make-Ahead Topping

Serve whipped cream topping without the last-minute fuss. Whip whipping cream; dollop onto baking sheet. Freeze firm. Transfer to freezer container. Cover, seal, label, and freeze. Top dessert with frozen dollops a few minutes before serving. Store topping no longer than 3 months.

Cool Strawberry Pudding Molds

⅓ cup sugar
4 teaspoons cornstarch
1 envelope unflavored gelatin
  Dash salt
4 beaten egg yolks
1¾ cups milk
2 tablespoons orange liqueur
1 teaspoon vanilla
4 egg whites
½ teaspoon cream of tartar
⅓ cup sugar
2 cups fresh strawberries *or* raspberries

In heavy saucepan combine ⅓ cup sugar, the cornstarch, gelatin, and salt. Combine egg yolks and milk; gradually add to gelatin mixture. Cook and stir over medium heat till thickened and bubbly. Cook and stir 2 minutes more. Remove from heat; cool slightly and stir in orange liqueur and vanilla. Cover surface of pudding with waxed paper. Cool to room temperature.

In mixer bowl beat egg whites and cream of tartar to soft peaks (tips curl over); gradually beat in ⅓ cup sugar till stiff peaks form (tips stand straight). Fold gelatin mixture into egg whites. Spoon *half* the mixture into twelve ½-cup molds; top with 1½ *cups* of the strawberries or raspberries and the remaining pudding mixture. Refrigerate for 3 to 24 hours.

Before serving: Unmold gelatin mixture onto serving plate. Garnish with remaining ½ *cup* berries. Makes 12 servings.

Chocolate-Coconut Dessert

- 1 6-ounce package (1 cup) semisweet chocolate pieces
- 1 13-ounce can (1⅔ cups) evaporated milk
- 1 10½-ounce package (about 5 cups) tiny marshmallows
- 1⅓ cups coconut
- 6 tablespoons butter *or* margarine
- 2 cups crisp rice cereal, crushed
- 1 cup chopped walnuts
- ½ gallon brick-style vanilla ice cream

In saucepan melt chocolate pieces in evaporated milk. Bring to boiling; boil gently, uncovered, 4 minutes or till thickened, stirring constantly. Add marshmallows; heat and stir till melted. Remove from heat; chill.

In skillet cook and stir coconut in butter or margarine till lightly browned. Stir in cereal and walnuts. Spread *3 cups* of the cereal mixture onto the bottom of a 13x9x2-inch pan. Cut ice cream in half lengthwise and then horizontally into 12 slices making a total of 24 pieces. Arrange *half* the ice cream over cereal. Spread with *half* the chocolate mixture. Repeat layers. Top with remaining cereal. Cover with moisture-vaporproof wrap. Seal, label, and freeze.

Before serving: Let stand at room temperature for 5 to 10 minutes. Makes 16 servings.

Ice Cream Éclairs

- ½ cup butter *or* margarine
- 1 cup boiling water
- 1 cup all-purpose flour
- 4 eggs
- 1 quart vanilla ice cream
- ¾ cup water
- ½ cup light corn syrup
- 4 teaspoons cornstarch
- 1½ teaspoons instant coffee crystals
- 1 tablespoon butter *or* margarine
- 1 tablespoon coffee liqueur
- ½ teaspoon vanilla
- ⅓ cup chopped pecans

Grease a baking sheet. In saucepan combine the ½ cup butter or margarine and the 1 cup boiling water; bring to boiling. Add flour all at once, stirring vigorously. Reduce heat. Cook and stir till mixture forms a smooth ball that doesn't separate. Remove saucepan from heat; cool slightly about 5 minutes. Add eggs, one at a time, beating after each addition till smooth. Continue beating till mixture is thick, smooth, and slightly sticky to touch.

Using about ¼ cup batter for each éclair, drop batter onto prepared baking sheet about 3 inches apart, leaving about 6 inches space between rows. With a small spatula, shape each mound into a 4x1-inch rectangle, rounding sides and piling batter on top. Bake in a 400° oven about 40 minutes or till golden brown and puffy. Remove to wire rack; cool.

Split each éclair in half lengthwise and remove webbing from inside. Fill bottom éclair halves with vanilla ice cream; replace tops.

Cover with moisture-vaporproof wrap. Seal, label, and freeze.

For sauce, in saucepan combine the ¾ cup water, corn syrup, cornstarch, and the coffee crystals. Cook and stir till thickened and bubbly. Cook and stir 1 to 2 minutes more. Remove from heat. Stir in 1 tablespoon butter, the coffee liqueur, and the vanilla. Stir in pecans. Cover and chill.

Before serving: Heat sauce, if desired. Serve warm or chilled sauce over frozen éclairs. Makes 10 to 12 servings.

Fresh Strawberry Frost

- 3 cups fresh strawberries
- 1 cup sugar
- ¾ cup orange juice
- 3 tablespoons lemon juice
- 3 tablespoons orange liqueur

In blender container place *half* of the strawberries, the sugar, orange juice, lemon juice, and orange liqueur. Cover; blend till smooth. Add the remaining strawberries; cover and blend again till smooth. Pour into an 8x8x2-inch pan; freeze about 2 hours or till partially firm. Break strawberry mixture into chunks; place in mixer bowl. Beat with electric mixer till smooth. Return mixture to pan; freeze at least 3 hours.

Before serving: Stir to break up frozen mixture. Spoon mixture into serving bowls or sherbet dishes. Makes 6 servings.

Grasshopper Parfaits

1 8-ounce package brownie mix
¼ cup chopped almonds
5 cups tiny marshmallows
3 tablespoons milk
3 tablespoons crème de menthe
1 tablespoon crème de cocoa
1 1½-ounce envelope dessert topping mix
⅓ cup crème de menthe
Whipped topping (optional)
Sliced almonds (optional)

Prepare brownie mix according to package directions, *except* add ¼ cup chopped almonds to batter. Bake according to package directions. Cool thoroughly on wire rack; crumble and set aside. In saucepan combine marshmallows and milk. Cook over low heat, stirring constantly, till marshmallows are melted. Remove from heat. Cool mixture, stirring every 5 minutes. Stir the 3 tablespoons crème de menthe and the crème de cocoa into marshmallow mixture.

Prepare dessert topping mix according to package directions. Fold marshmallow mixture into whipped dessert topping. Spoon alternate layers of marshmallow mixture and crumbled brownie into 8 parfait glasses, layering twice and drizzling about *1 teaspoon* crème de menthe over each brownie layer. Cover and freeze parfaits.

Before serving: Top each parfait with a dollop of whipped topping and sliced almonds, if desired. Makes 8 parfaits.

Very Vanilla Ice Cream

⅓ cup sugar
1 tablespoon all-purpose flour
⅛ teaspoon salt
1 cup milk
2 beaten eggs
⅓ cup vanilla liqueur *or* almond liqueur
1 cup whipping cream

Combine sugar, flour, and salt; gradually stir in milk. Cook and stir over medium-low heat till thickened. Stir about *half* of the hot mixture into the eggs. Return all the hot mixture to saucepan. Cook and stir 1 minute more. Remove from heat; cover and chill.

Stir the liqueur into chilled mixture. Whip cream to soft peaks; fold into chilled mixture. Turn into 8x8x2-inch pan. Cover; freeze firm. Break frozen mixture into chunks; turn into chilled mixer bowl. Beat till smooth. Return mixture to pan. Cover and freeze.

Before serving: Spoon frozen mixture into serving bowls. Sprinkle with ground nutmeg, if desired. Makes about 3½ cups.

Peanut Butter-Chocolate Bonbons

2 cups sifted powdered sugar
1 cup graham cracker crumbs
¾ cup chopped pecans
½ cup flaked coconut
½ cup butter *or* margarine
½ cup peanut butter
1½ cups semisweet chocolate pieces
3 tablespoons shortening

In large bowl combine the powdered sugar, graham cracker crumbs, pecans, and coconut. In a small saucepan melt butter or margarine and peanut butter; pour over coconut mixture. Stir till mixture is moistened; shape into 1-inch balls.

In another small saucepan over low heat, melt chocolate pieces with shortening. Spear shaped balls on wooden picks; dip individually into chocolate mixture to coat. Place balls on waxed paper; chill to set. Store candies, tightly covered, between layers of waxed paper in a cool place. Makes about 48.

Mulled Fruit Topper

1 8-ounce package mixed dried fruits, pitted and snipped
¾ cup water
2 tablespoons sugar
1 cup dry white wine

In saucepan combine dried fruits and water; bring to boiling. Reduce heat and simmer, covered, 10 to 12 minutes. Stir in sugar till dissolved. Cool slightly. Pour mixture into a jar with an airtight lid. Add wine, covering fruit. Cover and refrigerate at least 3 days.

Before serving: Spoon topper over ice cream or sponge cake. Makes about 2 cups.

Snacks & Beverages

Snacks, appetizers, and beverages are a pleasure to serve when you can prepare them in advance. Whether it's a party, a family get-together, or just an evening at home, make it easier with recipes from this chapter.

Included are snacks to serve at casual gatherings and more elegant appetizers appropriate to serve with cocktails. Choose a dry beverage mix that is stored on the shelf; add boiling water and it's ready to serve. Or, stir up a frozen drink that's served straight from the freezer as a slush.

These make-ahead snacks, appetizers, and beverages can be stored in the refrigerator, in the freezer, or on the shelf.

*Spiced Hot Chocolate Mix
(see recipe, page 91)
Beer-Cheese Logs (see recipe,
page 88)
Hot Fruited Tea Mix (see
recipe, page 91)
Stuffed Pasta Shells (see
recipe, page 89)
Spicy Snack Mix (see recipe,
page 90)
Caramel Corn (see recipe,
page 90)*

Snacks

Glazed Appetizer Meatballs

- 1 beaten egg
- 2 tablespoons milk
- 1 cup soft bread crumbs
- 2 tablespoons finely chopped green pepper
- 1 teaspoon salt
- 1 teaspoon Worcestershire sauce
- 1 pound ground beef
- ¼ cup cold water
- 1 tablespoon cornstarch
- ¼ cup red wine vinegar
- ¼ cup soy sauce
- 3 tablespoons brown sugar
- 3 tablespoons honey
- ½ teaspoon ground ginger
- ⅛ teaspoon garlic powder

For meatballs, in mixing bowl combine egg and milk. Stir in bread crumbs, green pepper, salt, and Worcestershire sauce. Add meat; mix well. Shape into 1-inch meatballs; place in shallow baking pan. Bake in 350° oven for 15 to 18 minutes or till done. Drain well.

Meanwhile, in saucepan combine water and cornstarch. Add vinegar, soy sauce, brown sugar, honey, ginger, and garlic powder; mix well. Cook and stir till thickened and bubbly. Cook and stir 1 to 2 minutes more. Cool slightly. Gently stir in meatballs. Turn into a 3-cup freezer container. Cover, seal, label, and freeze.

Before serving: Cook frozen mixture in saucepan for 20 to 25 minutes or till heated through, stirring occasionally. Serve with wooden picks. Makes about 42 meatballs.

● **Microwave directions:** Prepare the Glazed Appetizer Meatballs as directed at left. Turn into a nonmetal freezer container; cover, seal, label, and freeze. Before serving, place freezer container in a countertop microwave oven. Micro-cook on high power about 4 minutes or till partially thawed. Turn into a 1-quart nonmetal casserole. Micro-cook, covered, about 9 minutes or till hot, stirring mixture every 3 minutes. Serve as directed at left.

Pickled Fish

- 2 pounds fresh or frozen fish fillets
- ½ cup vinegar
- 1 4-ounce can green chili peppers, rinsed, seeded, and chopped
- ¼ cup cooking oil
- 1 tablespoon finely shredded orange peel
- ¼ cup orange juice
- ¼ cup chopped onion
- 2 bay leaves
- 2 cloves garlic, minced
- 1 teaspoon salt
- ⅛ teaspoon pepper

Thaw fish, if frozen. Place in 10-inch skillet. Add enough boiling water to cover. Simmer, covered, 5 to 8 minutes or till fish flakes easily. Drain fish; arrange in a shallow baking dish. Combine vinegar, chili peppers, cooking oil, orange peel, orange juice, onion, bay leaves, garlic, salt, and pepper. Pour over fish. Cover; refrigerate 3 to 24 hours.

Before serving: Drain off marinade. Cut fish into bite-size pieces. Garnish with orange slices, if desired. Serves 8 to 10.

Beer-Cheese Logs

Pictured on pages 86 and 87 —

- 2 8-ounce packages cream cheese
- 3 cups shredded sharp cheddar cheese (12 ounces)
- 2 tablespoons finely snipped parsley
- 1 teaspoon paprika
- ⅓ cup beer, warmed
  Sliced almonds, toasted
  Snipped parsley
  Fresh fruit or assorted crackers

Let cheeses stand at room temperature about 1 hour. In large bowl beat together the softened cream cheese, the 2 tablespoons parsley, and paprika till well blended. Stir in the shredded cheddar cheese. Gradually add warmed beer, beating till nearly smooth. Cover and chill mixture 1 hour. Divide mixture in half. With hands, mold each portion into a log shape; place on baking sheet. Insert sliced almonds in molded cheese, arranging as desired. Sprinkle with snipped parsley. Cover and refrigerate 2 to 24 hours.

Before serving: Transfer cheese logs to board or platter with wide metal spatula. Serve with fresh fruit or assorted crackers. (Dip apple and pear slices into mixture of water and lemon juice or use ascorbic acid color keeper to prevent the fruit from browning.) Makes 2 logs, 2 cups spread each.

Snacks

Stuffed Pasta Shells

Pictured on pages 86 and 87 —

- 1 8-ounce package (25 to 30) large shell macaroni
- 2 beaten eggs
- 2 cups ricotta cheese
- ½ cup finely chopped green pepper
- ¼ cup finely chopped onion
- ¼ cup snipped parsley
- ¼ cup milk *or* light cream
- ½ teaspoon finely shredded lemon peel
- ¼ teaspoon ground mace
- 1 15½-ounce can salmon, drained, bones removed, and flaked
- ⅓ cup fine dry bread crumbs
- 2 tablespoons butter, melted
- ⅓ cup grated Parmesan cheese

Cook macaroni, uncovered, in large amount of boiling salted water about 20 minutes or just till tender; drain. Rinse with cold water; drain. Set aside. Combine the eggs, ricotta, green pepper, onion, parsley, milk or cream, lemon peel, mace, and ½ teaspoon *salt*. Beat in salmon. Pipe or spoon into cooked shells. Place shells, filled side up, in a 13x9x2-inch baking dish. Cover and refrigerate 2 to 24 hours.

Before serving: Add 2 tablespoons *water* to dish. Bake, covered, in 350° oven 30 minutes. In saucepan combine crumbs and butter; cook and stir till browned. Cool. Stir in Parmesan; sprinkle over shells. Bake, uncovered, 5 minutes more. Serve hot. Garnish with marinated mushrooms, ripe olives, pickled hot peppers, and watercress, if desired. Makes 25 to 30 appetizer servings.

Layered Pâté Appetizer

- 5 slices bacon
- ½ pound ground veal
- ½ pound bulk pork sausage
- ½ pound ground turkey (1 cup)
- ⅓ cup dry white wine
- 8 ounces chicken livers
- 1½ cups sliced fresh mushrooms
- ¼ cup sliced green onion
- 3 tablespoons butter *or* margarine
- ½ teaspoon salt
- ¼ teaspoon dried thyme, crushed
- ⅛ teaspoon pepper
- 1 egg
  Lettuce leaves

Line an 8x4x2-inch loaf pan crosswise with bacon slices, letting bacon ends drape over edges of pan; set aside. In bowl combine veal, sausage, turkey, and wine; set aside. In skillet cook livers, mushrooms, and green onion in butter or margarine over medium-high heat about 5 minutes or till chicken livers are no longer pink. Stir in salt, thyme, and pepper; cool slightly.

Turn liver mixture into blender container or food processor bowl; cover and blend till nearly smooth. Add egg; cover and blend smooth. Spread *half* the liver mixture into prepared pan; top with all the veal mixture, then the remaining liver mixture, spreading evenly. Fold bacon ends over top. Bake, uncovered, in 350° oven for 1½ hours. Remove from oven. Cover top of pâté with waxed paper. Place another 8x4-inch pan and a weight (such as a can of vegetables) atop hot pâté. Drain off some of the juices, if necessary. Cool. Cover and refrigerate for 3 to 24 hours.

Before serving: Loosen edges of loaf with spatula; dip pan just to rim into hot water a few seconds, then invert pan and remove loaf. Slice; serve on lettuce-lined plates. Makes 12 appetizer servings.

Whole Wheat Rusks

- 2 cups whole wheat flour
- 1 cup all-purpose flour
- 1 teaspoon baking powder
- ¼ teaspoon salt
- 4 eggs
- 1 cup cooking oil
- 1 teaspoon finely shredded orange peel
- 1 teaspoon vanilla
- 1 cup sugar
- ⅓ cup finely chopped walnuts

Stir together the whole wheat flour, all-purpose flour, baking powder, and salt. Beat together eggs, cooking oil, orange peel, and vanilla; gradually stir in sugar. Add to dry mixture; stir till well blended. Stir in nuts. Spoon into two greased 8x4x2-inch loaf pans. Bake in 325° oven for 45 to 50 minutes or till done. Cool 10 minutes; remove from pans. Cool on wire rack. Cut bread into ½-inch slices. Place on ungreased baking sheets. Bake in 325° oven for 10 to 12 minutes; turn slices over and bake 10 minutes more. Cool thoroughly. Store in plastic bag or airtight container. Makes 32 slices.

Snacks

Caramel Corn

Pictured on pages 86 and 87 —

1½ cups sugar
1 cup packed brown sugar
⅔ cup dark corn syrup
¼ cup butter *or* margarine
1 teaspoon baking soda
1 teaspoon vanilla
6 quarts popped popcorn

In heavy saucepan combine sugar, brown sugar, corn syrup, ¾ cup *water,* and 1 teaspoon *salt.* Bring to boiling over medium heat. Boil vigorously, stirring frequently, till mixture reaches hard-crack stage (300°). Remove from heat; quickly stir in butter, soda, and vanilla. Pour over popped corn, stirring constantly till popcorn is evenly coated. Spread onto waxed paper. Cool; break into pieces. Store in airtight containers. Makes 6 quarts.

Honey Cereal Nibbles

6 cups puffed wheat cereal
2 cups peanuts
¼ cup sesame seed, toasted
½ cup packed brown sugar
¼ cup honey
¼ cup butter *or* margarine

In baking pan combine cereal, peanuts, and sesame seed. Combine sugar, honey, and butter; cook and stir over low heat till smooth and sugar dissolves. Pour over cereal; toss to coat. Bake in 300° oven 30 minutes, stirring occasionally. Cool, stirring occasionally. (Cereal becomes crisp upon cooling.) Store in airtight containers. Makes about 8 cups.

Crunchy Pasta Snack

8 ounces corkscrew macaroni
Cooking oil
½ cup butter, melted
¼ cup grated Parmesan cheese
⅛ teaspoon garlic salt

Cook macaroni according to package directions; drain. Rinse with cold water; drain well. Fry cooked macaroni, about 12 at a time, in deep hot oil (365°) about 1½ minutes or till evenly browned, stirring to separate. Drain on paper toweling. Repeat with remaining macaroni. Turn into bowl. Pour butter over macaroni; stir to coat. Combine Parmesan cheese and garlic salt. Sprinkle over macaroni; toss. Cool. Store in airtight container. Makes 4 cups.

Spicy Snack Mix

Pictured on pages 86 and 87 —

4 cups bite-size shredded wheat biscuits
2 cups pretzels
1 cup dry roasted peanuts
½ cup cooking oil
1 teaspoon chili powder
½ to 1 teaspoon bottled hot pepper sauce
½ teaspoon garlic salt

In 13x9x2-inch baking pan combine cereal, pretzels, and nuts. Combine oil, chili powder, hot pepper sauce, and garlic salt; drizzle *half* over cereal mixture. Toss. Repeat with remaining oil mixture. Bake in 300° oven 30 minutes, stirring every 15 minutes. Cool. Store in airtight containers. Makes 7 cups.

Sunflower Cheese Crisps

1 cup all-purpose flour
¼ cup butter *or* margarine
1 cup cream-style cottage cheese
¼ cup sunflower nuts

Combine flour and ¼ teaspoon *salt.* Cut in butter till mixture resembles fine crumbs. Beat in cottage cheese till smooth. Stir in sunflower nuts. Divide dough in half. On lightly floured surface, roll each half into a 16x12-inch rectangle. Cut into 2-inch squares. Prick each square several times with fork. Place on ungreased baking sheet. Bake in 325° oven for 15 to 20 minutes or till lightly browned. Place in freezer container. Cover, seal, label, and freeze.

Before serving: Let thaw at room temperature. Makes 96.

Pine Nut Snack

¼ cup pine nuts, peanuts, *or* pecans
⅓ cup creamy peanut butter
2 tablespoons corn syrup
1 teaspoon vanilla
1 3½-ounce can (1⅓ cups) flaked coconut

Spread nuts in shallow baking pan; toast in a 350° oven for 10 minutes, stirring occasionally. Set aside. Combine peanut butter, corn syrup, vanilla, and dash *salt.* Stir in coconut and nuts; mix till well blended. Shape into 1-inch balls. Store in airtight container in refrigerator. Makes about 24.

Beverages

Spiced Hot Chocolate Mix

Pictured on pages 86 and 87 —

5½ cups nonfat dry milk powder
2½ cups presweetened cocoa
     powder
2 cups tiny marshmallows
¾ cup powdered non-dairy
     creamer
3 tablespoons ground
     cinnamon

Combine nonfat dry milk powder, presweetened cocoa powder, marshmallows, powdered non-dairy creamer, and ground cinnamon. Mix thoroughly. Store in an airtight container. Makes 8½ cups mix.

Before serving: For one serving, combine ⅓ *cup* mix with ¾ cup *boiling water* in a cup or mug. Stir to dissolve mixture.

Hot Fruited Tea Mix

Pictured on pages 86 and 87 —

¾ cup instant tea powder
⅔ cup sugar-sweetened
     lemonade mix
½ cup orange-flavored instant
     breakfast drink powder
1 teaspoon ground allspice
¼ teaspoon ground cloves

Combine the instant tea powder, the lemonade mix, orange-flavored instant breakfast drink powder, allspice, and cloves. Mix thoroughly. Store in an airtight container. Makes about 1¾ cups mix.

Before serving: For one serving, combine *1 well-rounded tablespoon* mix with 1 cup *boiling water* in cup or mug. Stir to dissolve.

Vanilla Yogurt Sipper

1 cup light cream *or* milk
1 8-ounce carton vanilla yogurt
2 tablespoons honey
1 teaspoon vanilla
   Dash ground cinnamon
4 to 6 ice cubes

Combine cream, yogurt, honey, vanilla, and cinnamon. Cover; refrigerate 2 to 24 hours.

Before serving: Pour into blender container; cover and blend till combined. With lid slightly ajar, add ice cubes, one at a time, while blending; blend till smooth. Pour into tall glasses. Makes 3 (6-ounce) servings.

● **Chocolate Yogurt Sipper:** Prepare Vanilla Yogurt Sipper as directed above, *except* add ¼ cup *chocolate-flavored syrup* to mixture before chilling. Continue as directed.

Bubbly Fruit Refresher

2 cups unsweetened pineapple
     juice
1 6-ounce can frozen orange
     juice concentrate, thawed
1 tablespoon lemon juice
3 cups grapefruit carbonated
     beverage, chilled

Combine pineapple juice, orange juice concentrate, and lemon juice. Refrigerate 2 to 24 hours.

Before serving: For *each* serving combine ⅓ *cup* chilled juice mixture and ⅓ *cup* carbonated beverage. Serve over *ice*. Garnish with lemon wedges, if desired. Makes 9 (6-ounce) servings.

Frosty Eggnog Shakes

1 cup milk
¼ cup instant eggnog
⅛ teaspoon ground nutmeg
1 pint vanilla ice cream

In blender container combine milk, instant eggnog powder, and nutmeg. Cover and blend till instant eggnog dissolves. Add vanilla ice cream. Cover and blend just till mixed. Pour into a 3-cup freezer container. Cover, seal, label, and freeze.

Before serving: Let stand at room temperature about 20 minutes or till partially thawed. Turn into blender container. Cover and blend just till smooth. Makes 4 (5-ounce) servings.

● **Spiked Eggnog Shakes:** Prepare Frosty Eggnog Shakes as directed above, *except* add ¼ cup *bourbon, rum, or brandy*. Freeze and serve as directed above.

Fast Hot Beverages

Heat beverages in minutes using your microwave oven. Place the beverage in a nonmetal mug or cup. Cook in a counter-top microwave oven on high power about 1¼ minutes for 1 six-ounce serving, 2 minutes for 2 servings, and 3½ minutes for 4 servings or till hot. For 8-ounce servings, micro-cook 1½ minutes for 1 serving, 2½ minutes for 2 servings, and 4¾ minutes for 4 servings.

Beverages

Bloody Mary Mix

- 9 pounds tomatoes (about 30)
- ¼ cup lemon juice
- 2 tablespoons Worcestershire sauce
- 1 tablespoon celery salt
- 1 teaspoon onion powder
- ½ teaspoon bottled hot pepper sauce
- Dash ground red pepper
- Vodka

Wash tomatoes; remove stem ends and cores. Cut up into an 8-quart kettle. Slowly cook, covered, 15 minutes. (Stir to prevent sticking.) Press tomatoes through food mill to extract juice; measure 12 cups. Return tomato juice to kettle; stir in lemon juice, the next 5 ingredients, 2 teaspoons *salt,* and ¼ teaspoon *pepper*. Bring to boiling; boil 2 minutes. Cool. Pour into freezer containers, leaving 1 inch headspace. Cover, seal, label, and freeze. Makes 3 quarts.

Before serving: Thaw desired amount of frozen Bloody Mary Mix in refrigerator. For *each* serving, fill cocktail glass with ice; pour in *1 jigger* vodka. Fill with Bloody Mary Mix; stir.

Golden Fruit Punch

- 1 6-ounce can frozen orange juice concentrate, thawed
- ⅓ cup frozen pineapple juice concentrate, thawed
- 2½ cups water
- 2 sprigs fresh mint (optional)
- 1 12-ounce can ginger ale, chilled
- 1 pint lemon sherbet

Combine orange juice concentrate, pineapple juice concentrate, water, and mint, if desired. Cover and refrigerate 2 to 24 hours.

Before serving: Pour into punch bowl. Remove mint. Slowly add ginger ale. Stir with an up-and-down motion. Scoop sherbet into punch. Makes 12 (4-ounce) servings.

- **Golden Rum Punch:** Prepare Golden Fruit Punch as directed above, *except* omit ½ *cup* of the water and add ½ cup *rum* with the ginger ale. Continue as directed. Garnish with additional mint sprigs, if desired.

Hot Lemon Sangria

- 1 lemon
- 5 cups dry white wine
- ½ of a 6-ounce can (⅓ cup) frozen lemonade concentrate, thawed
- ¼ cup brandy
- ¼ cup sugar
- 2 inches stick cinnamon
- 1 lemon, thinly sliced
- 1 orange, thinly sliced

Cut 1 lemon into 8 wedges. Combine wine, lemonade concentrate, brandy, sugar, and stick cinnamon. Stir to dissolve sugar; add lemon wedges. Cover; let stand at room temperature at least overnight.

Before serving: Remove lemon. Cook over low heat till heated through. (Do not boil.) Remove cinnamon stick. Add fresh lemon and orange slices. Makes 11 (4-ounce) servings.

Apple Daiquiris

- 1 6-ounce can frozen apple juice concentrate
- ⅔ cup light rum
- 2 tablespoons lime juice
- ¼ teaspoon ground cinnamon
- 2 medium apples, peeled, cored, and cut up
- Ice cubes

In blender container combine apple juice concentrate, rum, lime juice, and cinnamon. Add apple. Cover and blend till smooth. With lid slightly ajar, add ice cubes, one at a time, while blending to make about 5 cups of slushy mixture. (If mixture becomes too thick before making 5 cups, add a little water.) Pour into freezer container. Cover, seal, label, and freeze.

Before serving: Stir mixture. Makes 6 (6-ounce) servings.

Spiked Tea Slush

- ⅓ cup sugar
- 1 tablespoon instant tea powder
- 1 6-ounce can frozen orange juice concentrate, thawed
- 1 6-ounce can frozen lemonade concentrate, thawed
- 1 cup vodka *or* rum

In a 6-cup freezer container combine sugar, tea powder, and 2½ cups *water*. Stir in the juice concentrates and the vodka or rum. Cover, seal, label, and freeze.

Before serving: Stir mixture. Spoon into chilled wine glasses. Makes about 11 (4-ounce) servings.

Index

Index

Index